A Moment's Peace

A Mom's Guide to Creating Calm Amidst Chaos

Elizabeth Irvine

ELIZABETH IRVINE

bright sky press
HOUSTON, TEXAS

2365 Rice Boulevard, Suite 202,
Houston, Texas 77005

10   9   8   7   6   5   4   3   2   1

Library of Congress Cataloging-in-Publication Data
Irvine, Elizabeth, 1962–
A moment's peace : a mom's guide to creating calm amidst chaos / by Elizabeth Irvine.
p. cm.
ISBN 978-1-933979-83-0 (softcover)
1. Relaxation. 2. Peace. 3. Motherhood. I. Title.

RA785.I78 2010
613.7'92—dc22   2009053990

Photos appearing on pages 22, 28, 36, 39, 41, 48, 50-51, 57, 60, 64, 90, 138 © Karen Walrond
Photos appearing on pages 12-13, 16-17, 20-21, 34-35, 42, 58, 71,74-75, 79,82, 86, 97,
100-101,110-111,116,118,119,121,128-129,133,137,144 © Karen Sachar
Cover illustration by Mike Guillory
Creative Director, Ellen Cregan; Designer, Wyn Bomar
Printed in China through Asia Pacific Offset

A Moment's Peace

A Mom's Guide to Creating Calm Amidst Chaos

ELIZABETH IRVINE

bright sky press
HOUSTON, TEXAS

Dedication

....

This book is dedicated to every mother who longs for a moment's peace.

TABLE OF CONTENTS

INTUITION

Can you be open to wonder?
Open to the idea that you may
know more than you think?

SERENDIPITY FEELS LIKE MAGIC.

When something in my
life happens by chance in a
beneficial way, it validates for
me that I am in my groove—
living in a way that feels
peaceful and contented.

BODY AWARENESS

The greatest instrument
I will ever own?
My body.
When given half the chance,
it knows what to do.

INTRODUCTION

Your turn for carpool. Dinner unmade. Orthodontist appointment started fifteen minutes ago. Cell phone vibrating. Conference call scheduled. Txt from husband: co. dwnsizing again. whos nxt? How can one more minute, and one more worry, be squeezed into your day?

If your life is anything like mine—and what mom's isn't?—at least some part of the scenario above rings some bells for you. What would you do for a moment's peace? Lock yourself in the bathroom? Leverage your house? Sell your soul? Anything? If you're an average mom, you need a moment's peace more than anyone else, and if you're an average mom, you probably feel like a simple moment of peace is also entirely beyond your reach. Let's face it, as wonderful as it is, motherhood can sometimes feel like a continual series of interruptions, your every thought and task fragmented as your attention is continually pulled in different directions. Not so unlike my experience—not only as a mother, but as a nurse in a large hospital working in the Neonatal Intensive Care Unit (NICU), the heart-wrenching section of the hospital that houses critically ill infants.

It was my first job out of college, and it was overwhelming. I was twenty-two years old, green, fresh out of school, and scared. The hospital was a place of great intensity, as everyone in the NICU was busy with their assigned tasks and I was just expected to perform. I guess it happened instinctually, just like being thrown off a dock in the deep end of a lake and being told to swim. There's no time to stop and think about the pros and cons of whether you know how to keep yourself afloat—you're operating on survival instinct. But as hectic and frightening as it was, those early days in my nursing career taught me a critical lesson: how to keep a cool head and allow intuition to move through me and get the job done. I quickly learned how to work carefully, efficiently, and diligently—staying calm amidst the chaos of beeping monitors, people shouting, and tiny infants needing care. In the NICU, I just did it.

I can still remember the yelling of orders, "start an IV asap and get that drip going now," also knowing I had to hook up the heart monitor on a different baby, check a temperature, suction…a list of 'to dos' so long that I teetered on the edge of feeling too overwhelmed to begin at all. There were so many critical tasks to perform, and so little time. When I think back on these days, it was as if I had a guiding presence, a blanket of calm control that seemed to instinctively wrap itself around me, allowing me to move swiftly and efficiently from one task to the next. This confident presence seemed to appear from somewhere deep inside of me, a calm voice whispering, just relax, focus on one thing at a time. Somehow I just got out of my own way, and allowed myself to be completely engaged but not panicked—to respond and not react, never stopping to consider that my actions bordered on determining the life or death of this innocent baby.

Actually, for me, motherhood doesn't feel so different in that although it's overwhelming and hectic, we find that we have the capacity to perform in ways we never thought possible. It makes me wonder, why is it we can be intuitive, rise to the occasion, or venture into new territory for the sake of our children and others, and yet never do the same for ourselves?

It was the birth of my third child that made me think about my ability a bit more—

as I again reached outside my comfort zone, first by making me expand the boundaries of conventional medicine. As a baby, my son Sam developed a challenging and rare skin disorder. Like with the NICU, this difficult situation spontaneously, intuitively forced me to gather up a confidence, a "knowingness," that things would be OK. It pushed me to climb through a portal to new possibilities, allowing me to help my son heal through living in a very natural, simple way along with using alternative medicine. This knowledge was a gift. Along with helping Sam, it also guided me to reclaim the innate wisdom that had been lying dormant in my body all along. It opened my eyes to a completely different world of possibility, one where the true nature of wellness became apparent, and self-care and a peaceful way of living became my touchstones.

You don't need to tell me: A mother's love reaches beyond any logical boundaries. Most mothers would sacrifice their very lives to protect the life of their child. How is it, then, that we miss the bigger picture, the weaving of our interconnected lives, in forgetting to nurture our own well-being? I believe it rests in our attempts to be selfless, quickly pulling on one thread instead of patiently working on an interconnected piece of art. In doing so, we somehow miss the beauty of the whole tapestry. In attempting to tend to everyone else first—when inside we are falling apart—eventually, over time, we lose our capacity to be strong for anyone. The good news is it doesn't have to be this way. We all have a choice. You have a choice.

When we choose to dedicate our time and intention to taking care of our self—effortlessly, our own self-nurturing reflects in our health, peace of mind, and joyful expression of life. This in turn emanates out to everyone we are near. If you are still thinking, 'I don't know if I can do that,' or, 'Putting myself first sounds selfish,' let me offer you an example most of us are familiar with. When you board an airplane with your children and the flight attendant talks about plane safety, she says in the event of an emergency an oxygen mask will drop down. Put yours on first and then secure those of your children. Why? Because you're no good to your kids if you're passed out in the aisle. Though this sounds extreme, so many of us are so crazed and busy that, in effect, we're already passed out in the aisle. In *A Moment's Peace* I want to offer you my strong belief that as mothers we need to nurture ourselves, and teach you how to get out of your own way, as I did in working at the hospital, and tap into your intuitive natural core of strength.

This can begin as you read these pages. As you read, try to create an uninterrupted environment and allow yourself to "feel" the words and images. When you begin to "read between the lines," perhaps you will get your first taste of feeling less tense and more relaxed and at ease. This experience you are about to embark on will gently take you by the hand and allow you to step into a new place. A space that is comfortable, peaceful, easy, and most importantly doable. It will teach you how to look at life with fresh eyes, empowering you to change the way you respond to your environment. Through techniques of breathing, body awareness, guided relaxation, and meditation you will learn the art of becoming more grounded and aware, opening you to your true nature more often. Find calm and clarity in the present moment. Explore alternative therapies. Discover what you love to do, tap into your intuitive self, and become more aware of your daily signposts guiding you along your way. We make our biggest shifts when we begin to weave these practices into our everyday. Life continues to bring me moments of joy and moments of chaos. For me, learning how to stay calm in the midst of chaos has been my refuge, and my secret. My intention in *A Moment's Peace* is to share that secret with you. I would like to guide you in changing even the smallest of habits, equipping you to create serenity in your life, every day.

Learning how to stay calm in the
midst of chaos has been my refuge,
and my secret. My intention in
A Moment's Peace is to share
that secret with you.

It isn't enough to talk about
peace. One must believe in it.
And it isn't enough to believe
in it. One must work at it.

— ELEANOR ROOSEVELT

Chapter One

WHERE DO I BEGIN?

Just for a moment, instead of the tornado of responsibilities, stress, and mayhem, imagine instead a deliciously calm sense of quiet. A whisper of grace. A space of serene, tranquility. Peace of mind. Stillness. Freedom. Strength. This is what a moment's peace feels like. This can be your everyday.

Everyday choices

I still remember one late springtime afternoon in which an everyday moment turned into a pivotal moment of choice—a moment that held the potential to turn on a dime into a completely different situation. This moment brought with it the opportunity to challenge me—to flex my muscle—in the "practice what I preach" mantra.

Busy with a day's work, I looked up and noticed my son standing next to me at my desk. I glanced over at the clock. In utter amazement, I squinted, re-reading the numbers; yes, it actually read 5:00 p.m. Where had the day gone? I felt like I'd just sat down at my computer. I then noticed my twin daughters, my husband, and our dog standing there—all of them appeared to be willfully looking around to see if there was any evidence of dinner being prepared. But as I looked over my shoulder and peered into the kitchen I saw nothing but clean countertops. No ingredients laid out for tonight's meal. Even the dog's dish was empty. Completely absorbed in my current project, I had lost track of the hours. How could it possibly be suppertime?

Noticing...

My initial gut reaction was one of frozen panic or "doe in the headlights." Next, slowly washing over me, I felt the shameful, powerful emotion of guilt. I grew aware that the muscles in my jaw, neck and shoulders were beginning to tighten like taut rubber bands ready to snap, sending a sharp ripple of tension throughout my body. As I noticed the sensations coming over me, I heard the "never enough time to do it all" motto beginning to echo in my head. I started to feel the heaviness, the pressure of orchestrating the feeding of our family as a mother's role, as my role, bearing down on me. And then I caught myself. I realized that I had a choice. This was that pivotal moment.

We have a choice

As I stopped myself, I felt a sense of relief. I felt grateful that I noticed. Through my years of practice, I knew that I had the freedom to make a choice about how to react to the situation. Rather than feeling pressure, guilt, or anger, I had the power to choose any path I wanted. Through my ever-evolving continual practice of self-awareness, I chose serenity. I chose to handle things with ease. Gracefully. It actually felt more like a natural instinct, which then somehow felt obviously clear and straightforward. Instead of a panicked race to the kitchen, I finished the paragraph I was working on, then stopped and closed down the work on my computer. Creating an atmosphere of calm, I slowly, elegantly, and with my head held high walked into the kitchen to talk with my family. With tranquil authority I told them if they were starving, to eat a piece of fruit or cheese to hold them over. Dinner would be ready at 6:00 p.m.

Change the direction of our lives

I opened the refrigerator door and luckily found a carton of eggs. I took my time and enjoyed whipping up an omelet. Everyone contributed to preparing the meal, from setting the table to organizing drinks or helping butter the toast. We all sat down together as a family for supper. I am confident my relaxed manner set the tone for all of us in enjoying this simple meal together. Alternatively, if I had reacted with a frantic, irritable, stay-out-of-my-way attitude, this same scenario held the potential energy to ignite a family explosion. Choosing this opposite approach could have set off the whole family into a full-blown spiral of roles and responsibilities, with everyone caught up in the thought of "I do more than you."

These key moments of choice are not easy. Though I have plenty of practice being mindful of these opportunities, I too continue to live with the daily challenge of creating appropriate, positive choices that bring peace, balance, and joy into my life and to those around me. Yet I find the effort absolutely worth it, and truly believe it is in the ordinary choices of our everyday that we begin to change the direction of our lives.

The other morning I was hurriedly moving along with the routine of getting children to school and adults to work, all on time. Job deadlines and school projects loomed while our dinner menu was discussed and lunches were packed. Feeling agitated with the demands and time constraints, my thoughts turned to the future when we are all out the door, instead of staying present with my task at hand. Later, I remembered the result of my distraction: my forgotten cell phone sitting on the kitchen counter, next to Sam's carefully packed lunch. Re-envisioning my approach for tomorrow—without succumbing to the pressures life can bring—I see my boy's lunch in his backpack and my phone in my bag.

Now it's your turn. Can you think of a situation that didn't go as well today as you would have liked? Re-envision the scenario, choosing to react differently to the situation. How would that choice have possibly affected the outcome? At the next opportunity, try to be mindful of your reaction, noticing, and making the best choice.

Your ticket home

Like Sam's illness provided me an opportunity to shift my perspective and live in a new way, the biggest problem in your life right now could actually be an opportunity, your version of my challenge, just waiting to lead you into a new place.

Think for a moment about something or someone in your life that drives you crazy, something that really makes you nuts or gets right under your skin. Have you got it? It's usually not too hard to come up with something. If more than one thing comes to mind (which can easily happen) just choose the first thing that came to you. If you are having trouble thinking of something, just relax and let your thoughts organically move to an issue, annoyance, or problem in your current life.

Know this very issue, this annoyance or problem, is actually your ticket to a better life. This situation is in your life, "in your face" for a reason. The reason is for you to discover, to learn, and to grow. This very issue is meant to prompt you to move out of your comfort zone, encourage you to step outside of your box, and nudge you to open up and widen your boundaries, uncovering and working through this very situation—something as severe as, does your husband or child drive you crazy all of the time? These big issues are usually what it takes for us to undertake a major shift. Once you've conquered the big ones, deal with everyday challenges, such as a loved one's occasional bad mood or tantrum, with more grace, deliberately. With time, it becomes almost second nature.

We must be willing to get rid of
the life we've planned, so as to have
the life that is waiting for us.
The old skin has to be shed before
the new one can come.

—JOSEPH CAMPBELL

Opportunity knocks

Albert Einstein knowingly reminds us "in the middle of difficulty lies opportunity." The first step in solving your problems is to acknowledge and own them. Stuffing the issues doesn't make them go away. Instead, they come out through your own behavior—be it anger or depression, or both. If you choose not to acknowledge your issues, problems, or annoyances—and that is a choice—the more they will continue to fester and ultimately lead you into deeper water, making things that more challenging in making amends or in making changes in your life that give you peace.

Becoming aware of what annoys us is the first big step. The next one is to create a solution. The solution may require that you stretch yourself in how that comes about, asking more from you or for something different than you have done in the past. Hopefully, the techniques in this book can move you on the path toward a solution. Through the idea and practice of present moment, or maybe through tools of relaxation, the goal is for you to build capacity to look at your problems with fresh eyes, and discover which of them can be solved simply through a calmer, healthier you. The famous quote applies brilliantly: "Change the things you can. Accept the things you can't. And have the wisdom to know the difference." Apply the following ideas in this book to help yourself in creating contentment, a freedom from wanting, and a peace-filled, joyful life.

I know these ideas and concepts can make a world of difference in your everyday because these beliefs are what I personally use. They are what work for me, and for thousands of others I have taught over the years. As you learn these techniques and become accustomed to infusing them into your day, life becomes easier. Life, and your experience in it, becomes a beautiful expression unique to you. Life doesn't change. You do. Be open and welcome in ease, peace, and a sacred connection with all things.

The Sufi mystic Rumi says of suffering:

Your defects are the ways that glory is manifested. Don't turn your head. Keep looking at the bandaged place. That is where the Light enters you. Find relief from your pain in this wisdom that your wounds of heart and body are portholes through which the splendorous Light enters you. Keep in mind that your wounds and defects may very well be the manifestations of the glory of God.

"The strongest oak of the forest is not the one that is protected from the storm and hidden from the sun. It's the one that stands in the open where it is compelled to struggle for its existence against the winds and rains and the scorching sun." — **Napoleon Hill**

To get you on your path, let's begin with the greatest instrument you will ever own— your very own body.

Awakening the intelligence of the body

It's kind of like magic. My body. It knows what to do, when given half a chance. It fights off invaders, rebuilds, purifies, produces elixirs of hormones capable of things such as making me happy or creating a baby; it turns the air I breathe into the perfect amount of oxygen and gets rid of the unwanted carbon dioxide, pumps purified blood to my organs, and the list goes on. Magically this all happens "behind the scenes." My body does all of this without my thinking consciously about it or commanding it to—and it is something even I take for granted. Until something goes wrong, that is, and I am forced to decode what happened, what caused a kink in this effortless, smart system.

Neon signs

When I come down with a cold, break out in a rash, feel sick to my stomach from overeating, irritable from lack of sleep, or stressed-out from worry—these are all neon signs, flashing like a freeway marquee trying desperately to get my attention. My body says, "Hey there, take a look at what you are doing—I am trying to keep things running smoothly, but come on, cut me some slack."

Likewise, when you get sick, become lethargic, or are just plain cranky, your body is trying to "talk" to you. It is your job to listen, to pay attention. And to make a change.

Respect the temple

My kids love to gently tease me because I refer to my body as a "temple." Whenever I am contemplating doing something not so healthy—be it working too much or eating too much ice cream—they chide, "Mo-om, remember, you always say 'don't pollute the temple.'" They have a good point; I take a respectful approach in caring for myself and my enthusiasm rests in the **place of prevention.** If I take good care, I allow my body's matrix to work as it is intricately, magically designed, and it responds in keeping me healthy and happy. My body is then allowed to rest in a place of true wellbeing. And, in exchange for my regular dedication of "paying in" to my personal health maintenance plan—I generally feel good. Feeling good translates to focused attention, endless energy, and an effortless peaceful presence. You don't need countless cups of coffee to keep you going; your body already has that capability buried inside. Peace of mind and tranquility are not an effect of being healthy—being healthy

gives you the capacity to achieve that moment of peace. And you don't have to twist yourself into a pretzel to achieve those effects (or completely give up coffee)—it can be as simple as taking a breath.

Relaxation in a nutshell

This breathing and body awareness practice is something you can do anywhere, anytime—in your home, on a bus, in an airplane, waiting for your turn in line. It is a valuable tool to help you get in touch with your own body sensations and allow you to notice feelings of discomfort as well as refine the quality of your concentration. Do this practice every day and your body will respond in a beautiful way. In this place of true wellbeing you too can experience increased energy, clarity, and feelings of peace and joy.

Keep in mind the key to this practice is to keep your awareness in the present moment—*noticing*, just as I did in the dinner example I gave you earlier in the chapter. As you begin this practice stay focused on each part of your body. As soon as you notice your attention becoming distracted, gently and firmly bring it back to your body and your breathing.

- **Get comfortable.** Begin by sitting or lying down. Either way is fine. Allow your attention to move to your natural breath. Simply notice that you are breathing.

- **Notice your breath** coming in, pause, and out. It's like welcoming in a best friend. Natural, easy, effortless, and relaxed. Put your hands on your belly and feel your abdomen rise and fall with your breath.

- **Become aware of your body.** Feel the contact of your feet with the ground. Feel your hips wide and level, shoulders back and down, head and neck in line with your spine, chin slightly tucked in so the back of your neck can be long.

- **Keep your attention** on what you can feel, your sense of touch. Bring your awareness to your toes. Allow your attention to rest here. Notice every part of your feet: heels, toes (start with your little toe and count over to your big toe), balls, arches, ankles, enjoy noticing your feet.

- **Now bring your awareness** to your shins, calves, knees, thighs, pelvis, and buttocks—noticing. If your attention wanders off, gently and firmly bring it back to your body.

- **Focus your attention** to the back of your body: your spine, shoulders, back of your head—noticing. Now bring your awareness to the front of your body: abdomen, lungs—noticing the rise and fall of each breath, perhaps the beating of your heart. Bring your awareness to your shoulders, arms, elbows, wrists, hands, and fingers. Bring attention to each finger, starting with your little finger and counting over to your thumb.

- **Bring your awareness** to the back of your throat, jaw, tongue, cheeks, eyes, then your forehead between your eyebrows. Be aware of the crown of your head. Feel your whole body, from the top of your head down to the tips of your toes. Feel how your body is interconnected. Your whole body. Return to your breath and deeply breathe in and out. Notice how you feel right now.

- **Rest in this feeling you have created, let it settle into you, wrapping around you.**

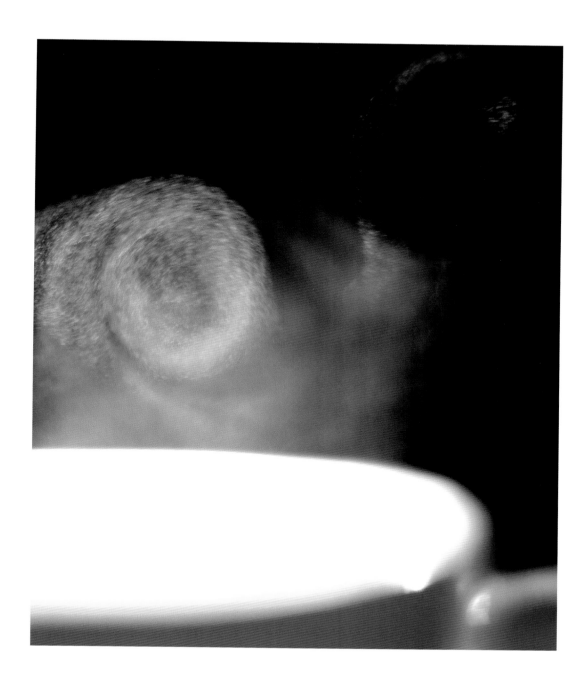

Chapter Two

....

PRESENT MOMENT, BEAUTIFUL MOMENT

Twenty minutes

How might you spend twenty minutes during your day? Sitting in traffic. Waiting for your dinner to cook. Listening to a co-worker expand on an idea. Reading a bedtime story to your child. Running a meeting. Folding laundry. Showering, dressing. As mothers, life might find us doing any of these activities. In fact, chances are we are doing more than one of them at the same time, hurrying, rushing. Life as a mother is busy whether we work in or outside the home. And if we allow this fragmented feeling to take hold of us, everything suffers: our health, our happiness, the natural joy of being a mom. By trying to be everything to everybody all of the time—eventually something's got to give. Often it's an illness, crisis, depression, or reaching a "breaking point" that forces us to surrender.

By living in a perpetual state of "doing" we create two problems, each of which leaves us with that familiar, nauseating "I can't do it all!" feeling. Trying to do it all, at the same time, creates a sense of constant chaos in our lives and for those around us. And the effects are even more far-reaching. This sort of crazed multi-tasking also means that we are not fully aware as we go through our days. Instead of feeling calm and powerful we only react to the world, dizzily spinning around in a revolving door instead of making our own choices and creating our own reality. **The good news is that each of us holds the possibility within us that any moment can become a peaceful moment.** And your reading this book indicates you've already made a decision to make a change for a healthier, more peaceful existence.

Still not convinced? Perhaps you are thinking, how can I possibly "survive" if I don't multi-task? Call to mind the last time you did something really well, something that made you really proud of your effort. Chances are you focused your energy into this one thing. Unlearning your mom habit of trying to do it all at the same time will help you achieve this feeling more often. And instead of suffering consequences from you taking off your supermom cape, your children will appreciate your undivided care when your attention is focused on them.

> Research by René Marois, PhD, says we consistently perform better and faster when tasks are done *successively,* rather than all at once. "A kind of bottleneck in the brain forces people to address problems one after the other, even if they're doing it so fast it feels simultaneous—it's like a mental traffic jam."

Shifting gears

Shift the gears from feeling pressured to perform and step into a new world, one fresh with subtle but powerful awareness in the present moment. Everyday life is chock-full of opportunity to live with mindfulness. Imagine life filled with blissful moments—for me, that can be as simple as noticing as the humidity lifts and I breathe in fresh, crisp air, or maybe it's truly enjoying my aromatic and flavorful lunchtime noodle salad. What I call "present moment" or mindfulness is really a simple three thousand year old Zen practice that is also referred to as mindfulness meditation, and it is a valuable gift you can give yourself.

The real world and real life

Harvard, Princeton, Yale and MIT have conducted more than 1,200 scientific studies that prove the numerous benefits of meditation. Why is it so many mothers don't practice meditation? Is it lack of time, interest, or understanding? For me, silent meditation is something I value so much that I carve out precious time every day for my practice.

WHAT IS MEDITATION?

Meditation really boils down to any activity in which you control your attention. Meditation includes mind-body techniques that help you feel relaxed and can even produce physical benefits, such as decreased heart rate, respiration rate and blood pressure. There are two general forms of meditation: concentration meditation and mindfulness meditation.

Transcendental Meditation

Transcendental Meditation (TM) is a popular form of concentration meditation. In this practice you sit in a comfortable position and focus your attention on one thing—such as your breath, or on a mantra, a sound or phrase that is silently repeated. A mantra can be a single sacred word such as "peace" or "Jesus" or "ohm" or even a whole prayer repeated over and over. The idea is to keep a passive awareness as you are the "observer" of your thoughts. If your mind wanders off to other thoughts or sensations, you gently and firmly bring your attention back to your breathing or your mantra. For best results, it is suggested to meditate twice daily for about 20 minutes. If you are just beginning, I recommend starting out with five minutes in the morning and then five minutes in late afternoon, gradually increasing until you reach approximately 20 minutes. Meditation can be as simple as dedicating five minutes lying in bed before going to sleep and five minutes after waking to do a body and breathing relaxation.

Mindfulness meditation

Mindfulness meditation is known as intentional moment-to-moment awareness, what I term "present moment." It is a non-judgmental awareness of your thoughts and actions throughout your day. Staying focused at your task at hand is an example of practicing mindfulness meditation: as you wash the dishes, focus on the soap and water cleansing the dish, notice if your mind wanders off to another thought and then gently and firmly bring your attention back to the fact that you are washing a dish. Mindfulness becomes a "moving meditation" throughout your day.

For some, and maybe you count yourself in this group, it may be initially breaking through the barrier of thinking that meditating is for gurus or is a granola-hippie thing, or thinking that you just don't have the right personality to be still. But meditation can be as simple as dedicating five minutes lying in bed before going to sleep and five minutes after waking to do a body and breathing relaxation. Another option, or a complementary idea to silent meditation, is the practice of "present moment"—mindfulness meditation.

I find that present moment is an effective way of quickly and surely pulling myself out of a frenzied, overwhelmed, "busyness" feeling. It enables me to step into a delicious sense of calm in its place. In time, focused attention becomes a form of "moving meditation," if you will. Because when my thoughts are scattered in several different directions, it's as if I am walking around half-asleep, functioning on automatic pilot. For example, have you ever driven somewhere and on arriving thought to yourself, how in the heck did I get here?

Put the idea of living with mindfulness into practice in real life and in the real world, because it works. It's a technique that lightens the load. Takes the weight off. It's about cultivating attention—an intimacy with awareness. Notice things as they are right now in the present, even "invisible" things normally taken for granted. Sometimes I simply bring awareness to my feet on the ground, or concentrate on the next breath I take in and out, or allow a passing thought or emotion (good or bad) to go through me without judgment. This change in perception is refreshing and alive and it becomes a powerful tool to de-stress and keep calm amidst chaos. One of the best parts about the practice of mindfulness—you can do it anytime, anywhere, and it's free.

I write for a health website's anxious and sleep-deprived audience. Scores of those readers have written to me about the benefit of incorporating mindfulness and relaxation techniques into their routine and tell me these practices helped change their lives. One reader told me, "These techniques help 'turn off' my mind or at least slow it down, so I can now sleep through the night." Another said, "Life feels calmer, I feel less worried, I am happier more often." In using these tools they are able to enter into a quieter place, and it becomes easier to still their thoughts and go and stay asleep. Life feels simpler, richer, and less stressful. Their overall wellbeing and health start to improve in miraculous ways. Yours can, too.

Looking for a needle in a haystack

Trying to find peace and calm by introducing a new mindful approach to living can feel like trying to find a needle in the middle of that proverbial haystack. In order to go forward, you first need to trust that serenity and joy are available. One of my favorite mindfulness

meditation teachers, Dr. Jon Kabat-Zinn, founding director of the Stress Reduction Clinic and Center for Mindfulness and author of *Where Ever You Go, There You Are: Mindfulness Meditation in Everyday Life,* explains how accessible it is. "You can't stop the waves, but you can learn to surf. It's not like you have to be a rocket scientist to learn this stuff, and it's not like you have to change your belief systems."

Start small and practice present moment "epiphanies." Simple everyday activities become "the material" to experience engaging in mindfulness in everyday life. Anytime becomes meditation practice. Before performing any of these daily activities listed below, catch yourself. Stop. Notice your feet on the ground. Notice your breath. Pause, take a deep breath in and out—then engage your attention in the task at hand. Notice how concentrating your thoughts changes how you feel as you perform the task.

- **Who's calling?** Before you pick up the phone or answer to your child's distressed call for attention.
- **Waiting in line.** Whether it's sitting in traffic, the carpool line, for the bus, or at the bank.
- **Mindful eating.** Notice what you are eating. Give your body the time it needs to digest. You will eat less and enjoy your food more.
- **Begin and end the day.** Notice upon waking or drifting off to sleep.
- **Walking anywhere.** Even if it's just to the bathroom.
- **Listen up.** Stay present in conversation. Just listen, who knows what you'll hear!

Learning to stay continuously focused in the present moment and on your task at hand can feel awkward at first, like anything new, but with practice it soon becomes second nature. Changing your habitual way of moving through the world not only will help you feel and function better, but your new awareness will show you how to turn time wasters into indulgent opportunities, creating a more effortless synergy with life.

PATIENCE IS A HARD DISCIPLINE.

It is not just waiting until something happens over which we have no control: the arrival of the bus, the end of the rain, the return of a friend, the resolution of a conflict. Patience is not waiting passively until someone else does something. Patience asks us to live the moment to the fullest, to be completely present to the moment, to taste the here and now, to be where we are. When we are impatient, we try to get away from where we are. We behave as if the real thing will happen tomorrow, later, and somewhere else. Be patient and trust that the treasure you are looking for is hidden in the ground on which you stand.   —Henri J. M. Nouwen

Practice tuning in

To begin, try using the kind of energy that you would normally use to do three things at once, and pour it, funnel it, into the present task at hand, be that making tea or working on a spreadsheet. My teenage memory of tuning into a radio station—attentively listening to the static as my fingers carefully turned the dial back and forth to get my favorite song to come in clearly—is an example of how this present-moment feeling happens. Keep "listening" until you get a sharp, crystal-clear signal. This "signal" is your awareness, your own diligently focused attention. And, this simple but ever-challenging Zen practice lightens the load. If you begin to practice this tuning in, every situation can be done with a calm, focused, and clear way of being—whether the kids can't find their shoes, your teen is running late, or the baby just threw up on your shoulder. Really.

In the rush of modern life,
we tend to lose touch with
the peace that is available
in each moment.

— THICH NHAT HANH

Everyday opportunities

This morning I took a shower. However, I wasn't really in the shower. My thoughts were already in the future, driving Sam to school, pondering what I would make for dinner, and then organizing my day's work schedule. Like many of us, I was nowhere near being present with the task at hand. By noticing my wandering thoughts and bringing my attention back to the shower, I began to feel the cleansing water's soothing sensation on my skin, allowing the warmth of the water to relax my stiff muscles. I became aware of the moist air, smelled the fresh mint scent of my shampoo as I massaged my scalp, and took in the aroma of my lavender body soap washing away the staleness of the previous day. This awareness became heightened and beautiful when I brought my attention back to the present moment. After my shower—when I'd truly stayed in the shower—I stepped out clean, refreshed, relaxed, and ready to greet the day.

Or, take another daily task, such as folding laundry. Envision what it feels like to fold it slowly, with love and care, acknowledging wandering thoughts, firmly guiding them back to your folding—taking pleasure in the softness of the fabric, the scent of fresh clothes, or gratitude for the moment here and now. We all know what it feels like to read your child's favorite bedtime story, for the umpteenth time. But think of the pleasure to be gained in staying focused on the words and story line, perhaps using extra emphasis on the characters' "voices," pointing out pictures, taking in the message that you are delivering, tenderly noticing your physical closeness. This is how this changes a chore into a special moment—a win-win for you and your kids.

The choice is yours, twenty minutes a day

Now that you get a sense of what you're striving for, it's time to put it into practice. Choose one daily task or activity. For one day, for a stretch of 20 minutes, practice fine-tuning your own attention. Whether that's laundry or dinner or a meeting or driving kids to baseball, bring yourself back to the task at hand when you notice a wandering thought. Make sure you take away potential distractions, such as your phone, the television, or email. Once you've practiced one task a day for a while, begin to notice how you are feeling when you stay present. Is there a noticeable shift? Are you more relaxed, energized? Does your new focused awareness bring you into harmony with who you are, your "new vibration" adjusting, and uplifting, you and those around you?

Next step, add in daily meditation

Now that you've noticed the difference attentiveness to the present moment can make as you go about your day, adding in the daily ritual of twenty minutes' guided relaxation—concentration meditation—is the next step to creating more peace and serenity in your life. Just as you diligently recharge your phone's battery or reboot your computer, this carved-out time is equally essential, giving you a tool to create a quiet, still space inside you and build capacity for tackling the unexpected. **Let go of any guilt for taking time for yourself.** In this place of uninterrupted surrender you rest, recharge, and bring clarity and joy into your everyday. You become the best version of you, and I assure you that it ripples out for everyone around you to enjoy.

BREATHING IN COLORS

Breathing in the colors of the rainbow is a simple and effective way to **treat yourself to a mini-relaxation.** Take a few minutes to practice now. In your imagination, hold each color individually in your mind and "breathe in" each color, one at a time. Begin with the color red. Breathe in the color red. Exhale as it fades away. Orange; breathe in the color orange. Exhale as it fades away. Yellow; breathe in the color yellow. Exhale as it fades away. Green; breathe in the color green. Exhale as it fades away. Blue; breathe in the color blue. Exhale as it fades away. Purple; breathe in the color purple. Exhale as it fades away. Look closely at the end of the rainbow. A pile of gold is shimmering in the sunshine. It feels like all the love and goodness in the world. Gold; breathe in the golden color. Exhale as it fades away. Think of a favorite color. Breathe in this color, soothing and cleansing. Exhale as it fades away. Notice how you feel? Do you feel relaxed, peaceful, energized?

Creating time and space for body and soul

One recent Saturday morning my teenage daughter Sarah was getting ready to leave for a weekend at her boyfriend's parents' beach house. She and I had discussed baking cookies for her to take with her as a token of appreciation for their hospitality. The day before, time slipped away, and at 8:00 a.m.—an hour before she was ready to set off—no cookies were baked. Typically, 8:00 a.m. is my "sacred hour." It's the time of day that slowly and gradually over the years has become my chosen hour to care for my body and soul—not for baking cookies.

Balancing time and space

Life as a mother keeps me flexible—continually willing to expand and contract. Schedules get disrupted. Plans get rearranged. Weather shifts, a storm develops or a rainy day breaks into brilliant sunshine. And, cookies get baked. Baking during my accustomed self-care time brought me two gifts. One, a taste of the love I hold for my daughter and two, the importance I place on my self-care. Motherhood is a balancing act. In order to keep myself in balance I rely on my devoted time every day using the tools of yoga and meditation to help me stay calm, flexible (physically and emotionally) and feeling good and comfortable in my own skin. As a mother it is easy to get trapped into feeling everyone else's needs come before our own. My sheer perseverance to routinely dedicate a part of each day to self-care puts me in a place of capacity. It creates a reservoir that I can pull from—a place that gives me physical and emotional "wiggle room," enabling me to do whatever happens to need to be done with a sincere and calm presence.

A dedicated time and space gives me a place to "be." Creating sacred space and an established time to my self-care welcomes in a ritual, a habit that at first softly whispered in my ear to come and use this time and space. Over time it has come to feel instead like it's dragging me by the arm, and my practice feels as necessary as the air I breathe. This particular day, the typically slotted "me time" got shuffled into another part of my day, an experience mothers know all too well. However, the capacity my daily practice created allowed me to feel good and welcome the time to spend with my daughter. In the beginning, I, too, felt guilty or awkward making sure I had this "me" time and there were plenty of days I let other things become the priority. However, over the years I have come to realize my carved-out commitment to caring for my body and soul gives me enough energy, clarity, and joy to nurture myself and still have plenty to share with those I love—whether I am baking cookies or not.

Creating a reservoir

Dedicating a piece of each day and finding a specific time helped me establish a routine. Over the years, my practice has evolved into an 8:00 a.m. slot—mostly because it's the time I am home alone, the house is quiet, and I am without distractions. The kids are at school. My husband is at work. My phone is turned off, my computer is sleeping. I know that emails can wait and make sure that meetings and appointments are all scheduled for after 9:00 a.m. For me, setting the same time and place each day to

dedicate to my self-care is a secret to my success, my commitment to show up and do it. The same time, same place scenario establishes a routine, a predictable security and comfort, and sets the tone and the pace for the day ahead. It has nurtured one of the best ways I know how to take care of me. I can still hear my Italian yoga teacher (almost fifteen years ago now) saying, "Elizabeth, remember this: Take the best part of your day, the time when you are most alert and fresh, and use it to practice. If you do this, everything else will fall into place." Her words still vibrate through me.

Setting the table

For me, another important part of my practice is creating a sacred space to practice. It's a bit like setting the table for dinner guests. When we have friends coming for dinner I always make an effort to add a little extra attention to my table. A fresh tablecloth, flowers, special napkins or maybe even crystal glasses. I intentionally create a beautiful place for us to share a meal, preparing the mood for a special dinner. Creating a special sacred place to take care of me is much the same.

Creating sacred space

I use a corner of my bedroom for my practice. I have a small trunk that serves as placeholder for a candle, a stick of incense, a cross, a plant, and a few photos—all symbols of the sacred for me. My yoga mat, a soft blanket (as our body temperature drops when we relax), and a chair (if I choose to sit in meditation) create my setting. To me, this space represents simple, safe, and sacred—a place that calls me in, sets the backdrop for my practice. Just sitting in this spot I feel peaceful and calm. My intention and invested energy in creating a dedicated space adds a special quality—it feels unique, serene, a holy corner of my bedroom.

Think about which room (or part of a room) in your home holds a special quiet feel to it. What does your current space need to create privacy, a serene and an uninterrupted refuge? Is it clean and welcoming? What can you do to make it sacred and beautiful? In regards to choosing a scheduled time—what hour of the day are you at your best? How does this time and place fit within your family's daily schedule?

SOME IDEAS TO GET YOU STARTED

- **Use your intuition** in helping choose the "sacred space" in your home.
- **Clear any clutter** from your designated area.
- **Collect a few things** to place near you that bring comfort and represent beauty or a connection to something beyond this world—the flame of a candle, a flower, a photo.
- **Set the intention** as you create your space that it holds a quality of "sacredness" as you practice.
- **Use this space** (if possible) exclusively for your practice.

Creating your sacred space is so important because, as author Denise Linn says in *Space Clearing A-Z,* "when we're in a place that is filled with Sacred Space, we feel better. We find it easier to breathe, think, dream, and to have faith in ourselves. The space that we occupy has a profound effect on us. Understanding this and learning how to transform ordinary environments into Sacred Space enables us to become powerful healers of your own homes and those of others."

SACRED SPACE

Why not create some alternative sacred space? Think about your garden. How about a chair and a beautiful cushion in a private spot, a cozy wrap to curl up in, and a small table to hold a few essentials—a simple vase with a single flower, a cup of tea, a journal. Or what about a view? Maybe it's a window view—a cozy bench, a quiet corner in the living room or a screened in porch—look for a pretty view and create the space. Think about your bath—soaking in an oasis of calm surrounded by candles, scents of essential oils, and sounds of silence. **Discover your own home through fresh eyes and create a sacred space just for YOU.**

You don't have to get naked: small steps to a place of quiet stillness
Incorporating the practice of mindfulness can feel foreign, overwhelming as an idea—and sometimes trying anything new can feel strange. It can feel like it's too big a deal to try it, so no bother in attempting. To alleviate stress and change the way we live, we have to be willing to try new concepts. Noticing things, such as our body sensations, breath or emotions

(without judgment), keeps us in the present moment. If we commit to diligently practicing these ideas, then gradually over time these practices become ingrained into our consciousness and into our everyday life. Eventually, this idea will begin to feel as natural as forming a smile or taking a breath. I am suggesting experimenting with an alternative option to coping with chaos and stress and busyness. I am encouraging you to try on a new coat, not strip down to bare skin. I am offering the idea of a new outfit—a fresh approach to daily wear and tear, with a closet full of new options.

Small steps to a better place

Finding your way out of an overwhelmed place happens in small steps. Adding lots of little steps together eventually leads you to a place where a clear, calm, positive mental attitude ripples out into every aspect of your life. Studies show that learning to still the mind, if only for a few minutes, can lower blood pressure, reduce heart rate, limit stress hormones, and enhance immune function. "Our modern world actually trains us to pay less attention and to become caught up in habits of worry and hurry," says Jeff Brantley, M.D., author of *Calming Your Anxious Mind: How Mindfulness and Compassion Can Free You from Anxiety, Fear, and Panic.* What's the antidote? Purposely pay attention to one thing at a time. "Being mindful is really just waking up with awareness and being truly present in your own life," Dr. Brantley says. "Whether it's becoming more aware of the sound and feeling of the computer keyboard on the pads of your fingers or enjoying the bittersweet, creamy taste of that iced latte you're sipping."

Assess where you are right now and how awareness and present moment might help you. Do you often feel like you coast through life on autopilot? Are you aware of your body sensations? What is taking place in your environment around you? Do you notice your thoughts? Do you live free of judgment? We all have room for improvement in making our present moment a beautiful moment. Start now.

Life can be found only in the
present moment. The past is gone,
the future is not yet here, and if we
do not go back to ourselves in the
present moment, we cannot
be in touch with life.

—THICH NHAT HANH

Does the thought of sitting cross-legged, eyes closed, chanting "auh-mmm" make you want to run and hide? Why not try out some of these "moving meditation" kind of mind-calming activities:

- **Tai chi.** This ancient Chinese practice is believed to offer all the health benefits of silent meditation, while giving you something to do with your hands and feet.

- **Take a walk.** Try taking a walk as if you had all the time in the world. Keep your steps steady and even. Keep your attentions on every step—heel, ball, toe. When you notice a thought (and they will come), bring your attention back to your feet and to the rhythm of your walking.

- **Rub a worry stone.** Why not? The ancient Greeks used worry stones to reduce stress. Find a special stone. Put it in your pocket and rub on it to help calm your frayed nerves.

- **Get out in nature.** Tune into nature's calming effects. Listen to an orchestra of birds chirping and insects buzzing, or take in the scent of heady wood or sweet-smelling grass, allowing them to transport you into a tranquil place.

- **Knitting.** What a great example of active stillness! Knitting is used in some hospitals to release stress. It is said that twenty minutes of knitting can lower your heart rate and blood pressure. Focus your mind as you go "knit one, pearl two" sliding the soft yarn around the smooth wooden stick. Nice.

Overdone

A first step in a fresh approach to bring a sense of calm into your everyday is transforming reality and your relationship to it. Disconnect everyday. Just for about 20 minutes. Just as I need to delete my cell phone's voicemails and my computer's emails, my brain needs to download some space. I need to **remove the constant contact.** Spending this time in silence reconnects me to another part of me. When I visit this quiet space regularly I make room in myself to serve others better.

Chapter Three

....

COMFORTABLE IN YOUR OWN SKIN

Promise me you'll always remember: You're braver than you believe, and stronger than you seem, and smarter than you think. — **A.A. Milne,** *Winnie the Pooh*

Have you ever had this thought—"I can't believe how silly I am to forget—the diaper bag, my cell phone, child's lunch on the kitchen counter?" or enviously compared yourself to the "other mom's" slim figure, clear skin, or radiant smile, or felt inadequately "over your head," overwhelmed with others expectations of you, work load, and maintaining a household? You are not alone.

Of course, almost everyone experiences negative thoughts, but a negative thought probably crosses your mind more often than you realize. Research says that the average person's brain has some 60,000 thoughts per day. Maybe more. And, unfortunately, research says that most likely 80 percent of these thoughts are negative. Immersing yourself in them can, in turn, lead to a critical lack of self-confidence.

Think for a moment about the last time you had a negative thought—about that slow driver or the pushy kid at the playground. Call to mind what happens when you re-visit this thought. Notice how it makes you feel. For me, negativity drags me down. It makes me feel heavy and drains my energy. Regrettably, that feeling is contagious; negativity has the capability of spreading like a wildfire catching on to dry grassland. Especially for moms, as many of our thoughts spiral along with how our children feel—how many of those 80 percent involve our kids?

Junk food fix

Am I good enough? How do others manage so much better than I do? Reacting from a place of guilty "shoulda, coulda, woulda" how can you deal with an overwhelming barrage of negative thoughts? The first step is to acknowledge that negative thoughts do exist. Begin to notice. When I catch myself in the act of negative thinking, it's kind of like noticing I've got my hand in the potato chip bowl, feeding myself a junk food fix. Splurging just happens and then later I wish I hadn't eaten it, maybe I even feel sick from indulging in food that's not very good for me. Just as junk food can create an ache in my stomach, negative thoughts make me feel equally unsettled.

Treadmill of pessimism

Unfortunately, one demoralizing, self-sabotaging thought can feed the next, keeping any of us on a non-stop treadmill of pessimism. These unwanted thoughts seem to turn up like an unexpected guest, and linger on. I am guilty of being tired and cranky, and no matter who in my family tells me to go and get some rest (just as I say at times to one of them) I can dig my heels in and tell myself I can ride out the storm of my bad mood—trapped in a glazed-over space of gloom and doom. Not only does that not serve me, it doesn't serve my poor family that has to deal with my bad mood. Over time, I have learned to surrender and say "enough is enough," and take care of me.

Freedom in choice

How do you move forward and leave negativity behind? The first step is to realize that you have a choice. No matter what life is dishing up—frustration, anger, disappointment—you are the only person who chooses your own thoughts and your reactions. Even prisoners are free to choose their own thoughts of peace under any condition. I often repeat Eleanor Roosevelt's famous quote, "No one can make me feel inferior without my consent" to myself whenever I catch myself thinking negatively. As mothers, especially, it is important that we allow ourselves compassion and generosity, not only toward others, but toward ourselves.

We are what we think. All that we are arises with our thoughts. With our thoughts, we make our world. —**Buddha**

Thought is the sculptor who can create the person you want to be. —**Henry David Thoreau**

It swings both ways

The good news is that although negative thoughts are contagious, the same is true of optimism. A positive outlook anticipates happiness, joy, and good health. Think of someone you know who is a positive person—how much fun they are to be around, how they lift your spirits and make you feel good. One way to remedy your own negativity is to spend time with positive people; besides being fun to be around, their way of being is catching. Have you ever noticed that when you are with a negative person you tend to feel tired or drained? Notice this feeling and you've taken the first step. The second step is to begin to place your time and energy with the people who bring out the best in you. Happy, comforting people are like a magnet, a mirror that attracts a reflection of happy and comforting. And, if you aren't already, soon you too can become one of these positive people that attracts supportive and encouraging friends.

How do I get comfortable?

Sometimes our underlying subconscious feelings of negativity can drag us down. Tools of creative self-expression can help unlock the door to what's on your mind—exercise, journaling, cooking, gardening, and dream diaries are just a few exercises that can uncover buried thoughts and feelings, allowing you to finally address what's really bothering you. Find the tool that works for you. No one technique is better than another. Try out different ideas and see which one resonates. Doing an activity that's enjoyable can help elicit a relaxed, comfortable feeling which in turn tends to loosen up underlying issues or uncomfortable thoughts that may be lurking just below the surface of our conscious mind. Uncovering subconscious thoughts is much like bubbles rising from a sparkly drink—they come to the top and then eventually lose their fizz, kind of like a natural expression such as a burp. It makes us feel better for clearing the space. When we uncover things that we previously had no idea were bothering us below the surface of our waking conscious mind, we make room for a clear and confident space, welcoming in plenty of room for peace and happiness.

> **Affirmation** (a declaration that something is true). Use affirmations to make a positive mental picture with your thoughts and words… "I see the best in everyone" becomes a mirror of what you attract.

Humanness is our power

As mothers, the only thing we usually have enough of is guilt, judgment, self-doubt—about us, about our kids. We're fed negative messages all the time. Having thoughts, positive or negative, is about being human. The trick to feeling comfortable in your own skin is becoming more self-assured. One way to do this is by beginning to notice your thoughts and then redirect them. As Elizabeth Lesser says, "'humanness' is our power. Drop through the rabbit hole and find ourselves a human being."

Like with present moment, awareness is key and it takes some dedication and practice. However, with patience and perseverance each step leads to a new you, creating a beautiful self-portrait and a positive self-image. As we move away from the negative, positive thoughts come more frequently, organically. In turn, slowly, but surely, we move into a confident space of increased positive thoughts and self-esteem. Your new gentle, but grounded, confidence allows others to feel good around you. As we let our own light shine, we unconsciously give other people permission to do the same, including other mothers around you and especially, your children.

BE A POSITIVE MAGNET

· **Make eye contact** and return greetings from others; be the first to say hello.

· **Give someone a compliment.** Everyone has something good and beautiful.

· **Focus on personal qualities you like about yourself**—such as your smile or your special way of doing something. Let your light shine.

· **Show an interest in others.** Ask about their homes, children, pets, hobbies, or travels.

Keep your thoughts positive, because your thoughts become your words.

Keep your words positive, because your words become your behaviors.

Keep your behaviors positive, because your behaviors become your habits.

Keep your habits positive, because your habits become your values.

Keep your values positive, because your values become your destiny. — **Ghandi**

Opportunities are always available for me to practice "getting comfortable in my own skin." This story, one I like to call "Sleep Over," is one such example of how I kept my thoughts positive, increasing my self-confidence as I grew through what could have been a negative experience.

In years past, whenever my husband was away, each of our three children would enjoy the tradition of a "sleepover" in my bed. Instead of being a lonely time for us all with Ron traveling, this tradition became an anticipated special time for the kids—equally welcome for me, too. Ordinary moments have the potential to become unique opportunities.

Mom and Dad's bed

The kids always coveted our bed. Mom and Dad's bed was much bigger than theirs and, unanimously, all three of them voted that our bed was definitely more comfortable. Sarah described our "soft sheets like silk against her skin," Allie felt "surrounded by a big fluffy duvet and enormous pillows," and Sam's tiny, tender head looked so small on top of it all. However, I think what all three of them loved most wasn't this bed fit for a king, but the special one-to-one time with Mommy.

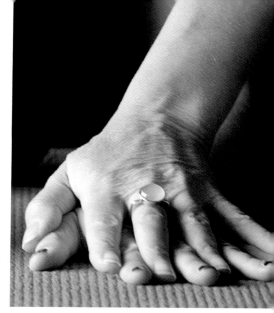

The warmth of human touch nourishes our soul

During those times each of my three children developed their own special cuddling tradition. Sarah was a hand-holder, interlocking her tiny, slender fingers between mine. Allie would nestle her head just below the bottom of my neck, resting in the flat, soft space of my collarbones. And my youngest, Sam, had a move that interlocked our ankles by resting his tiny foot on top of mine. We coined it the "foot wrap." All of these maneuvers were not so close as to be smothering, but just enough touch to feel the warmth of another body, the security that human contact brings, and a feeling of love that is unconditionally mother and child. This tradition went on for years, the kids rotating turns whenever Ron was away.

Time passes, opportunities change

One day, Sarah announced that we could skip her turn the next time it came up. She really no longer wanted to "sleep over." She liked the space of her own room and bed. My other two continued the tradition for another couple of years. Then, eventually, Allie, now entering puberty, let me know that her bed seemed just fine. She liked the idea of turning off her own light when she was finished reading, listening to her own music, having her own space. These things outweighed the idea of snuggling with Mom. No worries. I rested assured, as I knew lots of other mothers who had remarked how their boys had always been their "best" cuddlers. I relished the thought of the next few years of these occasional special nights with Sam, my youngest.

As mothers we need to give
our children the opportunity
to feel our unconditional love,
providing security for them
to be grounded and confident
within themselves.

No more foot wrap

Then the day finally came. My husband's business had taken him away from home for a couple of nights. I walked into Sam's room to say his prayers and kiss him good night. He didn't mention coming in for our traditional sleepover. I didn't mention it, either. I went to bed that night a little sad. Then, in the middle of the night, I felt the presence of him lying next to me. I started to wrap my foot around his. He whispered, "No foot wrap tonight, Mom. I need my space."

The next morning, over a quiet breakfast of Cheerios, Sam explained that he came into my room not because he missed our ritual but because he felt I was sad, and he didn't want me to be unhappy. I told him, thank you, that I would miss our sleepover ritual, but I understood he had outgrown our tradition. It was his time to have his own space. I could have let myself feel completely gutted and heartbroken—rejected, even guilty. Not only was I sad, but also my son felt the need to lift me up, even though it was something he didn't want to do! Instead, later that day I remembered something my mother (who raised nine children) had told me. As mothers we need to give our children the opportunities to feel our unconditional love, providing security for them to be grounded and confident within themselves. Instead of feeling sad or guilty, I felt proud I had raised independent, confident children. And I am continually reminded how I am challenged to keep growing right along with them.

How do we begin the shift, the process of creating a positive feeling? It's about learning how to raise our vibration.

Some mornings when I wake up to the rain falling, or the prospect of my day's busy schedule, I don't want to get out of bed. Ugh. It's morning already? Most everyone I know can relate to this feeling: I wish I could stay in bed, just a few more minutes...

A moment's peace

To combat the occasional morning blues, sometimes I like to pretend it's Sunday morning, even when it isn't. A wave of relief comes over me, oh-yeah, it's Sunday. Thank God. I roll over, snuggle in my soft sheets, comforting pillow, and let myself drift back into a blissful, peaceful rest.

Use this scene as an example to practice an exercise in feeling this moment. Think back to how you created a feel good sensation in the first chapter and begin to create this feeling in your imagination right now. Imagine your body is feeling relaxed and full of contentment. In this dreamy and stress-free 'moment,' your mind is relaxed, free of worry and frustration. Allow yourself the luxurious epiphany of a completely relaxed, content Sunday morning feeling. Let the feeling tickle you. No worry, no commitments, no place to be—only the quiet and loving space of your bedroom. Bring this feeling front and center into your awareness and settle into it. Wrap this sensation around you, covering you in a secure freedom. Allow it to permeate through you. Be confident.

Know that you can re-create this feeling anytime you want. Every moment, a moment's peace is available to you. The choice is yours. Focus your attention, and do it. Isn't that a better way to get out of bed?

Practice creating a feeling and learn to raise your vibration

Learning to create "Sunday morning" feelings gave me a tool to help myself. With practice, it becomes quite easy to re-create something that feels great—a relaxing body sensation, a wonderful sound, or a laugh-out loud memory. In doing this, I raise my vibration in attracting other positive vibes, people, and situations in my life—with the bonus of feeling good in my self. Here are some of my favorites—can you "feel" this?:

Sunbathing

One of my favorite childhood memories is one of climbing out of a swimming pool. Cold, shivering, and dripping wet I rest my slender young body onto the warm cement edge of the pool. I can still feel the heat of the concrete underneath me, the bright sun above me, sandwiching me in a blanket of bliss.

Cold, crisp winter

How about a briskly cold winter's morning? Ten years old and my dark blue wool coat, knitted gloves and hat provide a barrier from the frigid, icy wind ripping through the air. I happily walk on top of freshly fallen snow. Each step I take crunches a pathway for others to follow; breathing in, the crisp air tickles my nose.

An evening's fire

Sitting comfortably next to the glowing warmth and simplistic beauty of a fire sends a ripple of deep comfort through me. The smoke-filled air's heady, wood scent encircles me and makes me feel grounded.

Choose some of your own: Dig out a memory in the playground of your imagination

Turn back the clock and practice "playing" in your imagination. Create a feeling. You are the producer. You have endless resources of experience at your disposal. Generate a 'real life' fantastic sensation. Try it now.

- **Find a quiet space.** Get comfortable. Allow yourself the luxury of the next five to ten minutes to relax and dive into a feel good memory.

- **Relax.** Bring your awareness to your body and your breath. Use your breathing to soothe away any tension or stress your body is holding. Slowly breathe in a sense of ease. Deeply breathe out tension. Let a warm relaxed feeling begin to flow through you, cascading down from the top of your head all the way to the tips of your toes. Allow your mind to relax and your emotions to feel peaceful.

- **Call to your imagination.** Dip into your memory bank and withdraw an impression that managed to etch itself into your long-term storage. Find one that feels great. Perhaps you are in a beautiful place, with a good friend, or a happy and secure childhood moment.

- **Fill in the details.** Recall this experience. Stretch back into time and reach for that scene— look at the details. Where were you, what where the sights or sounds, who were you with, what was happening?

- **Remember how this felt.** How does it feel to be joyful? Do you feel lighter? A smile on your face? More energized? Try and describe what the feeling of joy means to you—open, clear, free? Take a few moments and bring your awareness to the sensations in your body. Allow these emotions to settle in. Breathe in this feeling of joy. Breathe out feeling relaxed, happy, and well.

Once you've created your feeling, stay with it. Linger on, massage it just little bit longer. If it's gone away, call it back. Are you able to get the feeling back? Can you coax it to you again, at will? The more you practice, the easier it gets. Try this exercise everyday for the next week. Soon you'll be able to slip into a good vibration without having to re-create every step. And that just feels good.

Vibrational essence of your desire

As a mother, I know that when I raise my vibration, I unconsciously welcome in a greater service to all who are with me. I can especially sense this within my own family—if I have a genuine smile on my face or have a sense of feeling good from the inside out, I send a strong wordless signal, a higher vibration, that effortlessly lets my family move through whatever they are feeling and gives them permission to resonate at a "higher vibration" too.

So even if it isn't Sunday morning, you know you have the opportunity to create the feeling—attracting all those good vibes right along with you.

> You will never reach the place where you will not need to be diligent about your choice of thought. Because you live in a world that is determined to show you every pocket of despair. So you must diligently choose. But it gets easier and easier and easier to do so. Right now, it may feel to you like those moments of connection are the rare ones. There will be a time when those moments of connection will feel so normal that it will shock you when you get into a place of disconnection. — **Esther and Jerry Hicks**

Darker shade of pale

Take a look in the mirror. I mean really examine yourself. I'm not talking about the façade of your natural complexion or the color of your eyes, but about going further inside, to a hidden part that isn't visible in your physical reflection. I challenge you, while your gaze is fixed there, to conjure up both the person you most admire and the one who drives you completely crazy—the boorish co-worker, your invasive neighbor, or a giving and dynamic girlfriend. Are there parts of you that you see reflected in those wonderful traits of your hero? If you are honest, do you harbor some of those very same negative qualities that make you dislike the other?

The people in your life right now, especially those you wish would just go away, can serve as hidden gems of self-awareness. How? Perhaps, we subconsciously attract into our lives the parts of us that we dislike the most. What if, unknowingly, we do this so we can experience and work on the part we don't readily acknowledge exists in us? What if subconsciously, you actually created and perpetuate the relationship drama, the grumpy child, the annoying boss, or the competitive friend? What if these people are presently in your life to help you understand your own potential equally negative or positive qualities? When we own up to our own traits, we move into a place of true compassion and understanding of our self and others and in our humility, we come into power.

Uncomfortable yet?

Can you see yourself? Can you imagine that you could be this person? Is there a tiny sliver of possibility that parts of you are also cranky, unfair, judgmental, stubborn, or maybe opinionated? Sometimes people or situations that make us the most uncomfortable are present because we need them as a catalyst to open us up, to "expose" the unpleasant idea that somehow we too are capable of the thoughts and behaviors we judge. Acknowledging this helps us understand our self from a different viewpoint, and asks us to learn and grow.

Aspects that are hidden from ourselves have a powerful influence on our present reality. They are always trying to get our attention in order to be accepted and integrated into our whole self.

— DEBBIE FORD,

author of *The Dark Side of the Light Chasers*

Do unto others

Do unto others is a message that withstands generations, holds the potential to unify political and religious borders and, a phrase comprehended (not always applied) from two to 102 years old—the golden rule: *Do unto others as you would do unto yourself.* As Atticus tells Scout in the classic novel *To Kill A Mockingbird,* "You never really understand a person until you consider things from his point of view... until you climb into his skin and walk around in it."

Look for the goodness

Look for the good in everyone. With gentle eyes, see the good in others' faults. Understand that you too are potentially capable (in some way) of being that person who annoys or seems disgusting to you—or is amazingly talented. If we can help heal a negative person or be genuinely proud of a gifted friend, then we are helping ourselves. Connecting to those whose faults drive us crazy, or embrace those, whose talents shine, allows us all collectively to heal; ultimately, we are all connected.

Embracing wholeness

I encourage and challenge you to embrace your wholeness: the emotions or traits you most fear or dislike in others, but also to learn to "own" your own positive traits.

Funnily, owning a positive trait can be uncomfortable as well. One common hangup is—the "not good enough" feeling—how many times have I heard or sensed it in myself? And, sure it can feel a bit scary to own your positive trait of being good enough. Practice recognizing your greatness. Acknowledging our gifts is just something we aren't told to do.

It shouldn't take another PTA mom to tell you you're a great organizer, or your kids to tell you you're worthy of love. Come back to the feeling of resting in a place of capacity as I talked about in the first chapter of the book—a place where you are more relaxed and life feels easier. Take a deep breath in and out and allow your breath to soothe you; now in this easier place, acknowledge both sides of you. Look at your negative qualities, they will allow you to deal with others with more compassion and understanding and own your best traits—depend on these positive traits to move more gracefully within yourself. Think about where you shine. Is it your dry-wit sense of humor, your stellar tennis skills, or maybe your comforting spirit? Claim and acknowledge your greatness—let it become more of you, more often, and use it regularly to your advantage. This is a great way to practice your new habit of self-awareness—catch yourself as you let your light shine brightly. Notice how good it feels and allow that light to illuminate you from the inside out.

Yin and yang

When we embrace both sides of our self, the negative, the positive, we become the definition of the Chinese belief in yin and yang: *"complementary opposites within a greater whole."* Think of it this way—if yin and yang are created together in a single movement, they are bound together as parts of a mutual whole. Just like the play of the tide in the ocean, every surge is complemented by a retreat. Or, to describe it another way, think of sunlight playing over a mountain. Yin represents the dark side. Yang represents the sunny side. As the sun moves across the sky, yin and yang gradually trade places with each other, revealing what was hidden and hiding what was revealed.

We are all made up of equally opposite traits. We are beautiful and ugly. We laugh and cry. We are capable of love and hate. When we learn to acknowledge the complementary opposites of our self, in our wholeness, we are peacefully free.

Only the lucky?

How is it some people seem to have a life where everything just "clicks" into place? We all know these people. Somehow they manage to get all of the lucky breaks, appear to step in all the right places, or gracefully smile when everyday irritations arise? Maybe you feel jealous, asking why isn't this life available to you and only to a precious chosen few? Maybe you even feel a bit of resentment when you are confronted with these "golden" people? Are these people just destined for good luck? Or are they making their own? Believing in yourself, trusting in your own capabilities, being comfortable in your own skin—that's the first step. Setting your expectations—and setting them high—is the next.

Ready to meet the unexpected

For me, finding peace and ease in life doesn't mean I won't come up against challenges. It means that in the midst of these things I can still feel grounded and calm and confident from a place of stillness deep within me. One of the tools I use every day is simply a matter of believing I have the necessary faith and intelligence to cope with any situation or circumstance the universe chooses to place in my path.

My life feels a mixture of pain and pleasure and a constant work in progress. Each stage of my life seems to bring with it challenges and rewards. Every single day I work on the values of "treating others as I would like to be treated," consequences of my actions, and being respectful to myself, others, and nature—whether my day involves talking out a teenage relationship drama with my daughter, taking refuge in my meditation, or dropping off the recycling. Yes, I love what I do. After twenty-five years of marriage I can say I still enjoy my husband's company, my body is healthy and I know how to make my mind feel deeply calm, my kids bring me joy and my work brings me deep satisfaction. However, life isn't always easy. It's not always calm and peaceful. Life brings me plenty of potential problems, situations, worries, and frustrations. Maybe it's missing an opportunity, or having a conversation that took a turn for the worse, or passing on an experience I thought I should have gone for, or watching my children fail at something. But, gratefully I can say I finally stand firmly in the belief that whatever situation arises—it is exactly what is meant to be unfolding. My conscious and subconscious thoughts are directly related and responsible for my experiences, and they are what I ordered.

Placing my order

I place a lunchtime order at my local café. I choose the veggie burger and fries. However, by the time my meal is served, I notice the Caesar salad at the table next to me. Changing my mind, I think, "Wow, that salad looks great." I now place myself in a food dilemma: enjoy my burger and fries and forget about the salad, or place another order for the Caesar and forget my burger. Burger, salad? The choice isn't really important; what matters most is that I enjoy the decision I make and take pleasure in my meal. No matter what I order, my confident decision brings ease (not only to my digestion) but to the degree of my enjoyment in this meal, and my life. Of course a lot of choices in life are not this simple, with greater ramifications, right?—changing jobs, choosing schools, moving house. But in some ways, maybe they are.

Simple and powerful, not always easy

Peace and clarity come from the freedom to choose my thoughts, to become the observer of my emotions, and allow my beliefs to rest in a place of non-judgment. This belief system allows me to feel powerful. It gives me the power of making my own decisions and the responsibility of living with the results. Your life, too, can really feel that simple. Return to the famous cliché, "Change what you can. Accept what you can't, and have the wisdom to know the difference." It's not just a cliché; it's a simple and powerful message.

Real life. Pause. Stop and rewind.

A few years ago, one of my dearest friends, Susie, lost her husband in a horrific helicopter crash. I remember one afternoon spent in her glorious English garden, sitting on a wooden bench holding hands. I was trying to make some sense of it all, searching for some way to bring an ounce of comfort to my gentle and beautiful friend, whose perfect family life with her two children had in an instant been turned upside down and dumped out into a new and very foreign existence. "Whenever you miss Mathew," I said, "when you are longing for his physical presence—stop, pause, and rewind. Notice the grass, the trees, the blue sky, or the birds singing—the physical beauty around you. Feel the magnificence, that you can see and feel and hear because Mathew is here—part of all this beauty and very much alive." I asked her to take comfort in nature's physical beauty—the moon, the flowers, the stars—because these things represent a place that all of us can always connect with. And, when we allow ourselves this luxury, this place to connect, we become part of everyone. "And, here lies comfort," I finished. "And here is your husband Mathew, smiling, always loving you." I spoke to Susie, whenever she found herself spiraling into sadness or frustration, to become aware of her emotions, acknowledge them, and then move on to a thought of gratitude for the brilliance of nature or for her children's unconditional love.

From a feeling of powerlessness, I could only offer her her own power to change her reaction to tragedy, and in that, I offered her everything. Instead of being angry or bitter, on the turn of a dime she is capable of becoming filled with faith; instead of feeling frustrated, full of love. Susie has the power to believe and have confidence in herself, and trust that she will gain strength and clarity every day. I asked her to allow herself to rest in this new poised optimism, to let this feeling settle in and become part of her. I quoted to her a beautiful thought from Max Ehrmann: "Be gentle with yourself. You are a child of the universe, no less than the trees or the stars. In the noisy confusion of life, keep peace in your soul." And as Susie and I sat together on that crisp sunny afternoon surrounded by deep natural beauty that felt more alive and beautiful than ever before, joined we became a strong and powerful force. We both knew it was going to take a lot of time for her to heal, but I also sensed a comfort rising from deep within in her, a core strength that appeared—such as the intuitive knowing that arrived back in my NICU days. This feeling showed up, one that either one of us may have doubted could every exist—our hands interlaced, connecting us to each other and to a world that had suddenly turned itself inside out, we sat in a deep and confident feeling—a " knowingness" that she was going to be alright.

I encourage you to recognize your innate ability to notice the present moment, live it to the fullest, and when your awareness rests here—be alive and taste it. You have the ability to place your own order everyday—and peace is always a choice on the menu.

Attention is the ability we
have to discriminate and to
focus only on that which
we want to perceive. The only
reason you are happy
is because you choose to
be happy. Happiness is a
choice, and so is suffering.

— DON MIGUEL RUIZ,

author of *The Four Agreements*

Chapter Four

SIGNPOSTS

Think enthusiastically about everything, but especially about your job. If you do, you'll put a touch of glory in your life. If you love your job with enthusiasm, you'll shake it to pieces. You'll love it into greatness! — **Norman Vincent Peale**

Your divine assignment

Why is it we can be intuitive, rise to the occasion, or venture into new territory for the sake of our children and others, and yet, be reluctant to do the same for ourselves?

I speak regularly to groups and during my presentation I generally ask the question, "Do you love what you do?" Rarely do many people raise their hands. However, recently there was an exception. I was speaking to the staff at a non-profit facility named the Devereux Network whose mission is *"a meaningful life for all people."* This center takes in and rehabilitates children, adolescents, and even adults that have emotional, developmental, or educational disabilities. That morning I asked the staff, "Who in this room loves their work?" The reply was unanimous: EVERY person in the room raised their hands.

This response was overwhelming to me. I speak frequently and *never* have I found a group of people who unanimously love their work. What was more remarkable was that the work these people do is trying, with great potential for burnout. How could it be? After my talk, my son Sam and I were taken on a tour of the campus. What struck me almost physically was the compassion and dedication of the teachers, counselors, physician, and administrators. Everyone I met had a very natural, effortless way of communicating their love of this place and their pride in the progress they made with these children. Literally, they were changing people's lives by helping individuals who, in all honesty, were probably headed for disaster.

Along with the numerous ways they rehabilitate their clients, the staff at Devereux makes a point to recognize each client's birthday with a party thrown by volunteers. Some of the kids couldn't understand why anyone would organize these parties for them. The reply was, by the time the clients leave Devereux, they begin to understand it stems from the same reason the staff love their jobs: "in giving we truly receive." The staff truly loved what they did, and felt richer for what it did for them to perform literally life-changing work. That experience will always stay with me.

So now let me ask you, Do you really love what you do? Are you raising your hand? If so, congratulations to you—keep on doing what you are doing and with a generous smile spread that goodness to everyone near you. If, however, you aren't overly enthusiastic about your work—whether that work is lovingly caring for your family and home, or being the CEO of a corporation—perhaps I can help you find your "divine assignment," the work that will make you love what you do.

Think about what you do every day. About which part of your day can you say, "I love it!"? When we spend more time doing the things we love—naturally, ease and comfort follow.

In giving, we truly receive

When I do something I love, I feel that "I am in line with the divine"—whether it is teaching, writing, hugging my children, or preparing a meal—they become a joyful expression, as they are all things I love to do.

- **Think about it. What do you like to do?** What did you used to do when you were younger, even a child, to feel better?
- **Where do you spend your free time?** Do you spend time doing things you love to do?
- **How do you feel?** When you do something you enjoy how does it make you feel? Do you lose yourself or lose track of time?

p you plug in to something new. Look to something you have never ⌐wer arranging, writing in a journal, or taking photographs. As you begin the ⌐ly lose any attachment to your end result—the outcome of your task. Reassure yourself that whatever becomes of your activity makes absolutely no difference. You are not trying to create a masterpiece; you are merely having fun, poking around a little with something new.

Choose a time and place to practice this activity when you won't be interrupted, and remove any potential distractions, so as to allow yourself the luxury of single focused attention. As you begin your activity focus your attention as if it were a very powerful laser beam. Stay with your complete attention on what you are doing and soon you will be able to feel the flow of creating in a space of the present moment—fresh and clear. If your mind wanders off your activity—gently, but firmly guide it back to your task at hand. A few signs that can validate you are "in your groove"—you lose track of time, maybe you find yourself smiling or humming a little tune, or perhaps you are creating faster and more effectively than ever before? It's OK to start your activity even in a bad mood—just begin.

Get your body out of the way so you can move from your soul. Spending time like this opens you up to your creative force, the place that is inside you, but can be resting dormant and untouched. Once you become familiar with how to gain access to this place, it feels more comfortable going there—which in turn leads to joy and peace in your life and to clarity about your own divine assignment. Ultimately, as you spend more time in any activity that you love, you are allowed to blossom into a life you love.

Serendipity

Recently I met up with a new friend for lunch: Sister Maureen, an ex-cop turned nun and founder of the Angela House, a halfway house for women who are released from prison. We shared lunch in a crowded lively bistro along with the staff clinical psychologist, Ms. Doyle. As we were all laughing away I realized their Irish sense of humor was much like my mother's—and I thought to myself, wow, Sister Maureen and Ms. Doyle are so much fun—and that is when it clicked for me. The combination of their names created my mother's name. Maureen Doyle! What is the chance of that? For me this was a serendipitous sign that I was in the right place, doing the right thing. Getting involved with this project was where I am supposed to be.

To me, just the word, serendipity—*the occurrence and development of events by chance in a beneficial way*—feels exciting and surreal. And, if I am doing what I love, it seems to attract ease to the way things unfold. Signs always manage to show up, not always as I may have envisioned, but they always appear.

Dragonflies

Serendipitous events guide me in going with the flow, creating ease in my life, helping me find my way—they lead me to finding what I feel is my divine assignment. They can also provide comfort and security, as I learned in my dear friend Lisa's reaction to my serendipitous encounter with a dragonfly. The following is an email I wrote to Lisa soon after she lost her father.

I took a photo of this incredible dragonfly that came across my path yesterday. It was huge and beautiful and magical. It prompted me to read about dragonflies. This is the message I took away.

The dragonfly is a symbol of change and being OK with it. It also represents our own personal light and transformation, and to Native Americans it represents a recent soul that has crossed over.

In dark, muddy water under a lily pad lived a family of water beetles. Once in a while, sadness would come over this little community when one of the water beetles, climbing up the stem of the lily pad to never be seen again. They knew when this happened their friend had died and they would never seem him again. One day, one of the smallest water beetles was determined to see the top of the lily pad. He promised to return. On top of the lily pad it was beautiful, warm and sunny. He was so tired and comfortable in the warm sun, he decided to lie down and have a little nap. He slept and his body changed. When he woke up he had shed his old skin, grew broad beautiful wings, a slender body for flying—he soared and saw beauty of a whole new world, he felt so happy and joyous with a way of being he never knew existed. Then he remembered his beetle friends, and how they were thinking he was dead, and they must be feeling sad. He felt more alive and better than ever before, that his life had been fulfilled instead of ended. But, his new body wouldn't allow him to go back under the lily pad into the water. His friends didn't know the good news. He understood that one day their time would come. So, he raised his wings and joyously flew off into his new life.

I thought you might enjoy sharing with the kids. With much love
—Beth

As my friend read this email, she later told me, she started to cry. Dragonflies have always been a favorite symbol of hers—she carries one on her keychain, in framed pictures, on plates in her house. She felt so moved by the symbolism in the message; she felt it was her father trying to communicate to her. I believe serendipitous events are moments of grace; they appear and act as ways to guide us.

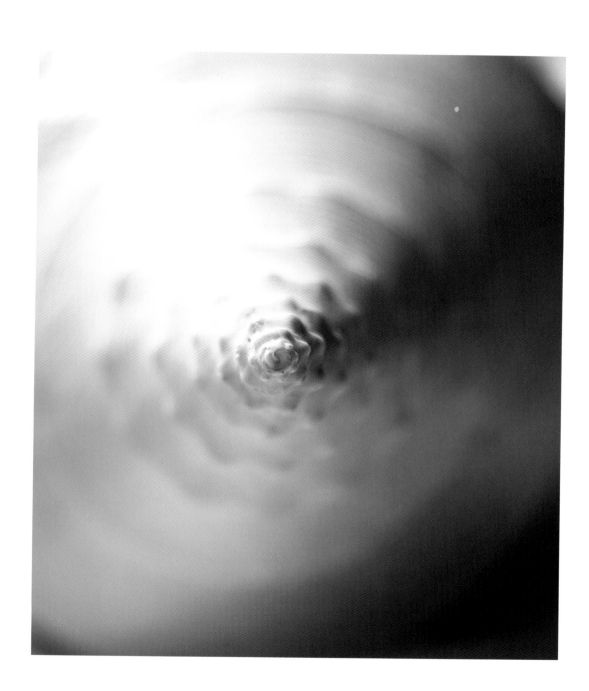

Instead of just thinking of
it as a coincidence, why not
allow a serendipitous event to
become magical, to validate
a feeling for you or to
bring you joy?

Signposts

Life brings signposts. If we choose to notice and acknowledge these serendipitous occurrences—it taps us into a whole new kind of tracking device, a tool to keep life on course. The development of events beyond my control can feel like magic. One day the famous rock group, the Beatles song *"Let It Be"* plays on my car radio, then in the grocery store, and again in an office building's elevator—it's too coincidental to ignore. It feels magical. I listen to the message.

An animal randomly crosses my path. It's easy to dismiss a butterfly landing on my shoulder or a hummingbird "humming" near my park bench as nothing. And, yet, it's equally easy to take notice. Why not take the experience of this animal coming into my awareness and use it? I look up the animal's symbolic meaning. Both of these creatures' symbolism rings true—a butterfly represents spirituality and a humming bird represents joy. It feels like I am hand delivered a note of inspiration, hope, and comfort. Can you think of a song, an animal, or any type of serendipitous event that's been in your life lately?

Turn ordinary into extra-ordinary

Obviously, serendipitous events aren't made-to-order. If I try to create one it then becomes meaningless. A mystical occurrence can appear like a flash of lightening or as a quiet whisper in my ear—whichever way it comes in, I am instantly transported from an ordinary moment into something extraordinary. They appear extra-ordinary or highly unlikely—and then again—as ordinary as a knock on my door. Playfully beckoning me to notice—nudging, encouraging me to follow along. And you don't have to believe in magic or the divine or some greater plan in order to recognize and let serendipity in. Instead of just thinking of it as a coincidence, why not allow a serendipitous event to become magical; to validate a feeling for you or to bring you joy? Recognizing these events and ensuring they are special to you is one more way you have power to create your own joy. Just keep it simple and fun, and perhaps just allow yourself to be open to the possibility that a signpost may be planted right next to you.

How many have I let slip away?

Serendipity isn't some exclusive club available only to a select crowd. These events happen daily and they happen to all of us—always available but only useful to those who notice. Before I signed the contract to write this book, my acquisitions editor and I had a long conversation in a lovely French café. Among other topics, we talked about serendipity, and she told me that the cardinal is always a good sign for her, guiding her along her way. I liked the idea of it, but told her that though we live in the same city, I never see them. The day I signed my contract, I walked out to get in my car, and a brilliant red cardinal was sitting on the hood of my car.

These occurrences make me smile. When they happen, it feels as if they take pressure off my life—as sometimes I feel like a tiny drop in an enormous sea. Instead of feeling insignificant with a powerful ocean around me—I embrace the possibilities of being connected to the source, and feel a deep and peaceful confidence within. How about you? Any of your chance happenings could be dismissed as nothing—how many have you let slip away?

KARMA: REAP WHAT YOU SOW

Karma originates from ancient Hindu philosophy and means, "the consequence of your actions." It is also found in the Bible: **"A man reaps what he sows"** (Gal.6:7, NIV) and in scores of other religious and philosophical traditions. In a nutshell, karma is the cause and effect of an action; it means whatever one chooses to do will define the experiences the soul must go through in the present life or future lives.

A universal law of cause and effect

According to James Van Praugh, author of *Unfinished Business*, Karma is neutral, "merely a tool for learning and having experiences. All choices are derived from either love or fear. Love is a pure high energy; fear is a lower fragmented energy. We often refer to these qualities as positive or negative." There is certainly no way to prove that Karma exists, but I do believe that things do happen as a result of the choices we make. Basically, we are responsible for our choices and the actions that our choices bring to us. We reap what we sow—good or bad.

> How people treat you is their karma; how you react is yours. — **Wayne Dyer**

Dream weaver

I have always been fascinated with dreams. Ever since my kids were little it's been a long-standing tradition around our breakfast table to share our previous night's dreams. It always makes for lively conversation, and it's a fun and interesting way for all of us to support each other and "crack the code" of what may be bothering us at a deeper level. I believe dreams are a pathway into our waking life, giving us messages and guidance to help us learn about ourselves—uncovering why we may be out of sync, or what issues are annoying us. Lots of the time our dreams hand us a much-needed piece of advice. Have you forgotten how to dream?

What is a dream?

Physiologically, dreams usually occur during the REM (rapid eye movement) stage of our sleep, which generally repeats in 90-minute cycles. That means you dream about every hour and a half, which begins as you drift off to sleep. Physiologically, we need to dream, as we need to discharge our "stuff" from the day. One of the reasons insomnia is harmful is because it deprives you of dreaming. If we can't "download" the events of the day we become edgy and nervous. On a more spiritual level, dreams can provide telepathic communication with others, messages from our higher self, our soul. Placing energy and intention to notice and reflect on our dreams can help us begin to break the perpetual "same old issue wheel" consuming dreaming and waking thoughts.

Inspirational dreams

Dreams can also bring powerful messages of inspiration and creativity. Albert Einstein's inspiration for the theory of relativity came to him in a childhood dream. In his dream, "He was riding on a sled that went faster and faster until it appeared to reach the speed of light. Everything was turned into beautiful colors and patterns and in that moment he was profoundly aware of the immense transformative power." He based his discovery of relativity, and felt his whole scientific career could be seen as an extension of this dream.

What about nightmares?

Along with discussing their best dreams, my children have always been able to talk about their nightmares, too. I can still remember the sound of their little feet racing down the hall as they came to jump into our bed if they had woken from a bad dream. Sometimes, they needed to discuss that bad dream right at that moment—but if I was lucky, we waited until breakfast. I told them not to be afraid, that their dream was a way of helping them. It brought to the surface and allowed them to see what was bothering them. Sometimes I had them draw the picture of their dream's scary monster in a friendly way—or we did a visualization where they could conquer whatever had frightened them. All three of my children have learned how to use a nightmare to face their fears!

> Your vision will become clear only when you look into your heart. Who looks outside, dreams. Who looks inside, awakens. — **Carl Jung**

O dreams; Keep me by you!
Let your soft-footed shadows carry me
Dancing through the midnight skies,
Laughing to the outer
edges of the universe.

— DENISE LINN

A great tool

My friend and mentor Denise Linn is an international lecturer, writer, and healer who among her numerous books has written specifically about **dreams.** She calls on her Cherokee Indian heritage and decades of experience in dream work and tells us that "dreams are messages from your subconscious mind and they are your greatest tools for understanding yourself and your life. Access this free source of inner power, wisdom and guidance."

Here are some of the best ways I know to get you started:

LEARN HOW TO REMEMBER AND USE YOUR DREAMS

- **Intention.** Tell yourself before you go to sleep that you will remember your dream.
- **Write it down.** Get into a routine of writing about your dream. Use a special notebook only for recording your dreams. Write it down as soon as you wake up. I do mine while I am waiting for my coffee to brew.
- **Remember the feeling.** What feeling did your dream create? How did you feel during your dream? What you are feeling in your dream is so important.
- **Give it a title.** Give your dream a one-word caption. This is your message.
- **Talk about your dream.** Use conversation. Share your dreams with your family or a close friend.
- **PRACTICE**

HOW TO DECODE A DREAM'S MEANING

- **Obvious.** What is obvious about your dream? What where you feeling?
- **Symbols.** Look at symbols in your dream. Are they common or universal? For example, traditionally water signifies emotions or feelings.
- **Dream Dictionary.** Create your very own dream dictionary. I feel the true definition of your dream can really only be interpreted by YOU. Keep a list of words, images, symbols that re-occur in your dreams. Write them down and look for a pattern, what they represent for you. This becomes your personalized dream dictionary to help you decipher the code.

Evidence of things unseen

What is intuition? A hunch, a gut feeling, a knowingness? Why are women notorious for having good intuition? Our intuition is like a built-in beacon that secretly guides us along our way.

In my experience on a general pediatric ward one day, I was filling out an admission form for a new little girl who had just arrived. Slotting the pieces together in the diagnosis puzzle—I asked the mother of the little girl, "Is her coloring and tiredness out of character for her?"

"My daughter always seems to be pale," she replied, clearly concerned, "but today she looks particularly ashen and her lips aren't normally this color. All she wants to do is sleep. I am so worried."

The mother's truthful feedback let me instantly know her little girl needed immediate attention. I quickly notified the attending physician and within hours, this little girl was in surgery for a heart condition. Picking up on the mother's genuine vibe of describing her daughter's norm allowed me to take a swift approach. Nine times out of ten, if mom said the child's indications were real, I already "knew" she was right. Think of something you "just knew." How did it feel when you knew without a doubt?

In *Blink: The Power of Thinking Without Thinking,* author Malcom Gladwell writes about a study that focused on nurses, intensive care unit workers, firefighters, and other people who make decisions under pressure. The study concluded that when experts make decisions they don't always logically and systematically compare all available options, as we are taught to do. Because in real life it all moves much too slowly. The study showed that nurses and firefighters would size up a situation almost immediately and act, drawing on experience and intuition instead to do their jobs.

Gladwell describes the concept of what he refers to as "thin slicing," the ability to tune in and focus on a few particular details, leading us to better decision-making than if we spend time to gather all the available information. Are you tuned in to your own intuitive powers? Do you allow yourself the power of "thin slicing" to help you day-to-day?

Inner compass

YOU have an amazing advantage to help you every day—your intuition. Tune into your own inner compass. Everyone has one. Our sixth sense is our very own personal guide, quietly waiting to be put into use in our everyday life. For some, this intuitive feeling rests in their heart, and for others the feeling settles into their gut. As the character Lily says in the *The Secret Life of Bees,* "The body knows things a long time before the mind catches up to them." Where do you 'feel' your intuition, your inner compass?

Exercising your intuitive muscle with your family

Just as I do yoga to keep my muscles fit—my intuitive muscle needs to be 'flexed' regularly to remain open and accurate. For me, intuition means paying attention. Can you think of some big decisions you've made based on your intuition? Can you think of times when you didn't listen to your gut, and wish you had? Using my sixth sense works best when I heighten my awareness to my other five senses as well. All of my senses are meant to complement each other and I use them as a checks and balances' system.

Observe your child in a new way

As with present moment or noticing, tuning in to your inner compass gets easier with practice. To get started, try this exercise with your family. Take a moment to notice the contact of your feet with the ground. Pause, breathe, become quiet—now check in with your heart, or your gut feeling —look at your children. One by one, with keen awareness, soften your gaze, and with a heart filled with compassion listen to what they have to say. Observe their tone and their mood. Use a very subtle noticing. It is not about assuming, judging, or criticizing. With continual practice, this technique evolves, and you will quickly learn to 'read between the lines' and pick up on faint and subdued messages your kids are subconsciously sending. As you become more grounded and familiar with this way of 'noticing', your clarity improves, the signals gets louder and you gain access to a place that has always been available to you—just undiscovered. This very subtle but always present information complements your intuitive "knowingness," and it can allow you to help your child in ways you never before imagined.

Sonia Choquette, in *The Intuitive Spark,* says using our intuition as mothers can help us stem problems with our children before they blossom into something uncontrollable. "Parents who are aware and connected to their hearts will notice when a child's vibes are off-key. It usually begins with a subtle shift; many times parents will ignore it, wanting more concrete proof that something is wrong. However, if we'd stop doubting our wisdom, and instead trust our intuition, many problems could be corrected before they got out of hand."

Believe in YOU

Can you be open to wonder? Open to the idea that you may know more than you think? Why are we so quick to follow the advice of our family, friends, authority figures, even talk-show hosts on TV, others who we imagine have so much more knowledge than we do? The plain and simple truth is YOU are the only one who knows the truth of what's best for you. The hardest part of owning this concept is getting out of your own way so you can get in touch. There is a boundless space that connects you. Look for that uncomfortable nudge, a "something doesn't feel quite right" notion, or perhaps an unexplainable feeling to take a different path. These are signals, your intuition trying to alert you. And just the opposite, if you are getting a deeply confident, peaceful feeling don't question it. The trickiest part of learning to trust your vibes is that your feelings won't always give you **the message you want to hear or believe,** but they will always lead you to the truth. Einstein sums up the feeling well, "When the solution is simple, God is answering."

Put it into practice with pen and paper

Let's dip back into the idea of love what you do and use the following exercise to help with some direction in discovering what you may not realize brings you joy, or help in making a current decision in your life. Use this exercise to tap into your own intuitive wisdom and hear what the "voice of your soul" is telling you.

Let's do it

Go grab a piece of paper and a pen. Let's do this exercise right now. Take a moment to center yourself,—feet on the ground beneath your feet—pause, breathe, smile, and now allow yourself the luxury of a few minutes to ponder a concern or ask for insight. Formulate your question. Write it down. Getting your question down on a piece of paper sort of "cements" it into your subconscious.

Bring your awareness to your body, your breath, and relax into your quiet space. Keep all of your attention on your breath, follow your breath's rhythm, deep, slow and steady. Allow any worry, tension, frustration, or anger to leave your body through your breath. Now recall your question, and hold it in your mind. Repeat it to yourself a few times. Notice if you have any feelings bubbling up? Notice what you are feeling—are you resisting this process? Jot down any thoughts you can feel, describe them. Come back to your breath; use your breath as your anchor (feel it sinking, connecting you to the sea's floor) until you feel relaxed and calm. Use your breath to sink deeper into either your heart or your "gut" (your belly just below your navel).

As you get more relaxed, bring your awareness to the end of your exhalation and rest in the space at the end of your exhalation. Ask your ego to leave and your high self to enter. Ask your question. Now, wait in your quiet still space—without any expectation—and see what surfaces. Remember, your answers do not always come as you imagine. Your answer may come as a feeling, an image, or even a conversation with someone a day or two later.

It may be a good idea to spend some time in nature after you "plant a question." Nature is non-judgmental, it's a place where we can feel safe and disconnect from our day-to-day worries, and more receptive to hearing our guidance.

Pay attention for the day or two after you formulate your question, as you may be surprised at how your intuition comes in. Once you have "planted your seed" of a question in your subconscious, pay attention to your results. Write down insights that come to you. Let these insights percolate. As they do, YOU begin to subconsciously create shifts in the background of your mind without even realizing it. Always remember that negative insights—such as blame, judgment, or anger are not coming from your higher self. The last part of this exercise is to take your answer or your insightful message and put it into practice!

A couple of final thoughts to consider

Intuition is subtle, unseen, and easily dismissed as "nonsense." For me, the word non- "sense" is literal; it means that you are not paying attention, not utilizing all of your senses, forgetting about your sixth sense. Remember when using your intuition not to try too hard. Once you shift your awareness to the fact that you are tapping into your instinct, intuition usually comes without your invitation. You are welcoming an intuitive feeling, not commanding one.

How can we avoid being misled by our intuition? I like the sound advice of Larry Dossey, MD, author of *The Power of Premonitions,* "In non-emergencies, we should rely on multiple sources of information—logic, reason and analysis, plus intuition. Multiple strands of information help guard us against bad decisions. When we rely on only one source of knowing, we can get into trouble. This is common sense: Don't put all of your eggs in one basket." Your intuition is an incredible gift. And typically as mothers, we are utilizing this place every day, though perhaps unknowingly. Go ahead, tap in and get started, and flex your intuitive muscle.

The best and most beautiful
things in the world cannot
be seen, nor touched…but
are felt in the heart.

— HELEN KELLER

Chapter Five

TOOLS OF YOGA: BODY AWARENESS, BREATHING, AND RELAXATION

Creating some space in your reservoir

Our body is just like a reservoir. Living in a place of capacity is about creating ways to "lower" the level in your own personal reservoir so that you may stay in a **place of prevention.** In this place of capacity you create a buffer around yourself, a divine shock absorber, allowing room to maneuver a little more gracefully through life. I encourage you to keep some space in your reservoir and leave room for the unexpected.

Awaken interest and curiosity

For me, yoga began with going to a weekly class and learning the postures, breathing, and relaxation. The beginning days of learning to yoke or "join up" my mind, body and spirit, slowly and surely over the years has edged its way into my life, creating a place of true well-being for me. Looking back on those initial yoga classes, I realize how that first step was such an important one. Now my healthy lifestyle is a way of life, and it penetrates every aspect of my being. Following are some simple, basic principles to awaken your interest and peak your curiosity of how to reconnect to your intrinsically natural way of being.

Our body is an amazing tool

Gentle yoga stretches, breath work, and relaxation are three powerful tools that make up the practice of hatha yoga, a practice that is meant to bring balance and harmony to your body, mind and spirit. Those tools have become as essential and regular for me as brushing my teeth or washing my face every morning. My practice gives me a way to tap into a place that allows my body to self-heal. Learning to relax my body, and therefore my mind, also creates a quiet, still space. In this place my body can reconnect, recharge, and renew, and I have more capacity to deal with whatever life deals me.

If you dedicate the time to practice every day you too will begin to see a real difference, increased energy, a sense of calm, and more joy. Yoga is not an exercise that asks you to wear special clothes, hang out with an incense-burning crowd, or become vegetarian. It can begin as simply as taking some time to explore the idea of focusing your attention in a new way. You can wear your p.j.'s, relax in a quiet space and count your breaths, or try out some gentle stretches with focused awareness in a pair of jeans, or sit and quietly meditate on your bus ride home.

I began with a weekly Wednesday morning gentle breath-based yoga class in a local activity center—on Wednesdays I felt fantastic, and so I kept going. What I am suggesting is you decide what might work for you—what you can do to ensure that you will begin to

care for your body and soul. And if that means a morning walk while focusing on each step in connection with your breath, or any of the other numerous suggestions made earlier in the book—then step in and begin. Whether you gingerly slip your big toe in or jump in with both feet. What I can say, is that once you get a taste for the good feeling of caring for YOU can bring—be prepared to continue, as your body and mind will crave the repercussions of balance—ultimately healthier, happier and more at ease in this new and better place.

The following poses, breathing exercises, and relaxation technique are only meant as a taster, a sample to get you started. Nothing beats a certified, enthusiastic, compassionate teacher to guide you on your path. I frequently remind women the best way to find a class that fits is to make it convenient, and resonate with your teacher. If you aren't too sure about the class, keep looking—the good news is you can sign up for a yoga class almost anywhere: a local gym or YMCA, a studio, or a church hall.

Yoga is not a religion. It does not require you to believe in a certain God or to chant mantras. It's an ancient science, which leads to health in the body, peace in the mind, joy in the heart and liberation of the soul. — **H.H. Pujya Swami Chidanand Saraswatiji**

Yoga Poses

"Undoing my body"

In my practice I am continually refining the quality of my attention. Intently focusing on my body awareness, breathing, and then the etched-out quiet space—this allows me to dig down deep and "undo my body." It's as if I chip away at the build-up, the stress, and the wear-and-tear of everyday life. I feel my practice isn't optional, it's a requirement if I want to continue to live in a healthy and happy way. Sometimes this daily commitment and process can lead to an unexpected outburst of emotion. This surge of energy cannot be easily explained—a burst of crying, a headache disappears, an annoying specific muscular tension leaves—it's almost like it's a discharge of built-up pressure. When I unite my mind, body, and spirit I gain entry into the subtle yet highly intricate matrix of self-healing.

My "essential" everyday yoga poses

For me, simple yoga poses are just as powerful as the more challenging or difficult postures—as long as they are practiced with focused attention and grace, and done with stability and ease. Following are some of my essential everyday yoga poses.

BASICS THAT APPLY TO EVERY POSE

Begin and end every session with a short relaxation—even if it's just a few slow calming breaths to center yourself. Set the intention to shift gears and enter into a time and space dedicated for self-care.

Hold the pose only as long as you feel a beautiful stretch, and you enjoy it. Listen to your body. Come out of the pose when you lose concentration, or it begins to feel uncomfortable. Allow yourself time and attention, watch and wait for your body to respond. Remember the goal is not the glory of the pose.

1. Mountain Pose: *ground and center yourself*

This pose brings a state of concentration, calmness, and awareness to your practice. Begin by standing with your feet hip-width apart. Bring attention to your feet. Spend a few minutes letting your toes ripple on the floor. Place one toe down at a time. Feel both feet with equal amount of weight. Bring your attention to your pelvis—open and wide, attention to your shoulders—back and down, and attention to your chest—open and soft. Keep your chin slightly tucked in so your neck can be long. Focus your eyes upon something in your vision at eye level. Bring attention to your breath. Watch your breath as it gently comes in and out. Feel and imitate the qualities of a mountain... grounded, still, powerful, majestic.

Mountain pose, done correctly, is a foundation of yoga postures This position helps correct your posture—it allows you to hold yourself with grace and dignity. It's a great way to give your body a break from the stresses of the day, with the bonus that you can practice this posture anywhere, anytime—standing in line, preparing a meal, taking a shower.

2. Forward Bend: *"quick fix" anytime during your day*

This pose is an inverted pose, meaning your head is upside down. This is great for allowing more blood to your brain, and improving your circulation. It also improves digestion and keeps your spine supple. The most important thing to remember regarding this pose is that it doesn't matter how far forward your body bends. Begin by exhaling. Bend forward from your waist until your back is flat, allowing your hands to come toward the floor, letting your head follow. It's like you're bending as a hinge from your hips. Go as far as is comfortable. If your hands do not reach the floor, use a chair or cushion to support your hands or elbows. Hold this pose only as long as you're comfortable. Bring your attention to your feet, heavy and strong on the ground. To come back up to standing, place your hands, palms together, on your chest and slowly, gently come up one vertebra at a time, so the last thing to come up is your head, allowing your spine to follow you to standing. Stand for a breath or two and notice how your body feels. Are you refreshed?

3. Child's Pose: *relaxes your sciatic nerve*

This posture is a wonderful stretch for the spine; it relaxes the sciatic nerve that runs down your legs from your spine and is a good resting pose. Kneel down and sit back on your heels. Bend forward from your waist and stretch out your arms in front of you. Stretch from your hips all the way to your fingers. Feel your tummy resting on your thighs, forehead resting on the floor. Breathe in and out through your nose. Stay in this pose as long as it feels good and your concentration remains on your posture and your breath. This pose is a counter-pose for the Dog.

4. Dog Pose: *best bang for your buck*

This is an all-round great pose for posture. It allows your spine to release, therefore adequately supplying blood to spinal nerves. It is also an inverted (upside down) pose, so it gives the head a fresh supply of blood, which is great for improving your circulation, clearing your mind, and keeping your skin healthy.

   Imagine a dog stretching its spine. Begin on your hands and knees. Your hands and knees have become the paws of a dog. Tuck your toes under, exhale, and raise your hips toward the sky, allowing your spine movement to extend from the hips. Your head hangs down, following your spine. If your legs do not fully extend, that's all right. Use slow and smooth, focused breathing. Take care not to strain your hamstrings, the muscles at the back of your legs. Stay in this position for as long as you are comfortable.

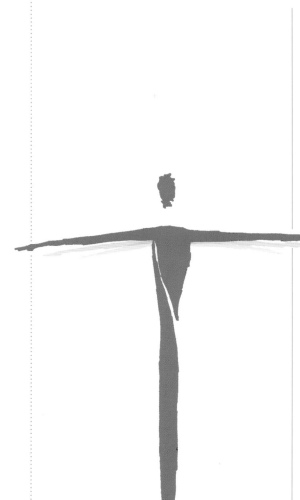

5. Standing Twist: *squeezes fresh blood supply to your body*

This pose helps with your spines flexibility and tones your spinal nerves. It also naturally massages the abdominal organs and regulates the secretion of adrenalin. Begin standing with your feet hip-width apart. Bring your awareness to your feet, heavy and grounded. Feel your feet sinking into the floor. Gently allow your arms to swing from side to side. Focus on your breath and letting go of the muscles in your lower back. Be patient—don't twist too hard. Breathe, watch, and wait for your body to respond. Feel this twisting as a very natural motion. Think heavy base, light upper body. Stay with it as long as your attention stays on your twisting!

6. Standing Balance: *brings clarity to your decision-making*

This simple balance is fantastic for developing your concentration and decision-making skills. It requires an even distribution of your weight on both feet. Begin standing with your feet hip-width apart. Bring your awareness to your feet, heavy and grounded. Interlock your fingers and stretch your arms above your head with your palms up toward the ceiling. Fix your gaze on something at eye level. Bend your body first to the right and then to the left. The movement should come from your waist. Try 10 times to each side. Now rise up on your toes and bend to each side 10 times. Ask yourself a question. Did the answer come easily and with confidence?

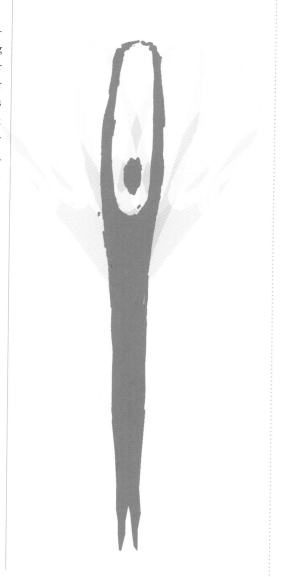

Breathing

Intelligence moving inwards

The "magic" of what happens when we can allow our minds to remain focused on the simple beauty of the breath is incredible. Personally, I feel it is like being told a really good secret, something I had always known but didn't remember or know how to use, like having a built-in defense mechanism in my body that was just lying dormant, just as I talked about accessing your intuition earlier—available but untapped.

One of my yoga teachers, Sandra Sabatini, describes it this way in her book *Breathe the Essence of Yoga:* "Gather all the senses that are usually extended towards the outer world and turn them within. It is intelligence moving inwards. During the day you use intelligence to catch words, to grasp messages, to listen, to filter emotions. You don't need to do that now; use that intelligence, that capacity to listen to what is taking place inside. The inner eyes are looking at what takes place inside; the inner ears are listening to the breath."

Putting it into practice

I have chosen two of my favorite and most frequently used breathing techniques to share with you. These two methods are what I use personally and teach regularly. With any breathing technique there are a couple of things to remember. "Breathing normally" means breathing in and out through your nose with your mouth lightly closed. Our nose filters out impurities, adds the correct moisture, and adjusts the air temperature so that we get the best quality of air into our lungs. After knowing this, why wouldn't you want to breathe through your nose?

You can lie down (if you feel tired) or sit (cross-legged, sitting on your heels or in a straight back chair) to do your breathing exercise. Either way is fine—most importantly keep your spine straight and not rigid, allow your body to be relaxed and your mind alert.

The "magic" of what happens
when we can allow our minds
to remain focused on the
simple beauty of the
breath is incredible.

Abdominal breathing, *quickest single thing you can do to relax*

Abdominal breathing is the quickest, single thing you can do to relax your body and therefore your mind. I use it constantly in my private practice of teaching others how to relax.

Bring your attention to your breath. Follow your breath, and allow your mind to be the observer, watching your breath coming in and out. Place your hand on your abdomen with your thumb on your navel and let your other four fingers fan below. Feel your breath in your abdomen, and notice how your abdomen is gently rising and falling in rhythm with your breathing. As you breathe in, your abdomen rises. As you breathe out, your abdomen falls. This takes some concentration. It becomes easier with practice. Focus on your natural rhythm, smooth and effortless, breathing in and out. Let your breath soothe you, taking you to a place of comfort; the thoughts of the day disappear.

Add counting

Adding counting is another option when practicing abdominal breathing. It allows you to occupy both sides of the brain, right and left hemispheres. In doing this, it keeps you completely focused on your breathing. Start with the number nine and count each inhalation and exhalation as one cycle or round. Count backwards to zero. As you progress, you can increase the number. If your mind wanders off, gently bring it back and start over with your counting.

Add a mantra

Another option that helps you stay focused is adding a mantra. This time imagine there is a line that connects your navel to your throat. As you breathe in, your breath travels from your navel to your throat. As you breathe out, the breath travels from your throat to your navel. Add in the words SO-HUM. Breathing in from your navel to your throat, you say the word SO; and breathing out from your throat to your navel, you say the word HUM. In Sanskrit SO-HUM means "I am that" beyond the limitations of body and mind, at one with the absolute.

Alternate nostril breathing

This technique involves breathing with one nostril at a time purifying the channels in which energy/air flows. This exercise creates a state of calmness and tranquility. The flow of breath is equalized. It cleanses the blood of toxins. It relieves pressure from the forehead and if you have ever happen to get a headache this technique can make it disappear. Begin by sitting in a position that you are most comfortable in (as described in sitting breathing), most importantly with your spine straight. Place your thumb and fourth finger on each side of your nose, and let your other fingers rest on the bridge of your nose. Breathe in through one nostril while blocking the air passage from your opposite side. Now inhale from one nostril and exhale from the other; inhale from the second nostril and exhale from the first (closing and releasing nostrils with your alternate thumb or finger). Breathe slowly, softly, evenly, and deeply. This is one round. Repeat for five cycles, increasing to ten when comfortable. If it seems too complicated to use one hand, try using both hands, and cover alternating nostrils with index finger from right and left side

FINDING A QUIET STILL SPACE

Act a little less and think a little more. Work your eight hours or your 10 hours or your 16 hours. Just spend at least 10 or 15 minutes—in a day where you are working 8-10-16 hours of physical action in order to maintain the physical stuff that you've gathered around you—trying to find pleasure from some vision. Afford yourself that. And that 10 or 15 minutes that you are finding pleasure, will cause a focalization of energy within you that the Universe will actualize around. You will begin to notice that you are more productive, because of 15 minutes of visualization, than you were from 16 hours of hard labor. — **Esther and Jerry Hicks**

Learning to relax and let go

Antar Mouna Sanskrit translation is "Inner Silence"

Following is my "tried-and-true" relaxation technique known as "inner silence." This is a variation of a technique I learned through the Bihar School of Yoga in Munger, India. I have taught this technique to thousands of people, empowering them with a way to let go of physical tiredness, mental tension, and move into a quieter still space.

Let me teach you how to relax

Begin by lying down symmetrically, your head and neck in line with your spine. Allow your legs to turn out with your feet naturally turning outward. Place your arms down by your sides and let your palms face up, your shoulders rotating back and down into the ground. Allow your head to turn slowly side to side and then come in line with your spine, your chin slightly tucked in so your neck can be long, and stretch. Focus your attention on your sense of touch. Take your mind rhythmically through the different parts of your body that are touching the mat: your feet, pelvis, shoulders, and the back of your head. Feel Earth's gravity pulling the tension from your body, allowing your body to release tension and tightness.

Awareness to sense of hearing

Next bring your attention to your sense of hearing. Listen for all the sounds you can hear. Listen for loud sounds and soft sounds. Choose one sound and listen to only that sound, excluding all others.

Awareness to your breath

Now bring your awareness to your breath. Just simply notice that you are breathing. You can say to yourself, "I am breathing in and I am breathing out." As you focus on your breathing, breathe in and out through your nose with your mouth lightly closed. Keep your jaw soft, your throat soft, and your lips lightly touching. Notice your inhalation and your exhalation. Watch with keen attention, focusing only on your breath coming in and then your breath going back out again. Focus your attention on your breath in your abdomen. Place your hand on your abdomen and begin to notice the movement of your hand with the rhythm of your breathing. As your hand rises, feel your inhalation, and as your hand falls, feel your exhalation. Keep all of your attention on the movement of your hand synchronized with the rhythm of your breathing.

Begin with five minutes of practice a day
Stay with this practice for five minutes and then gradually add in five minutes more until you reach twenty minutes. Many physiological changes take place as your body begins to relax. Begin to notice how you feel after you relax.

QUICK FIX: RELAX AND JUST BREATHE

Breathing and visualization techniques to stay centered. Try out this simple exercise. Whenever you find yourself stressed take a few moments to be with your breath. Simply lie flat with your hands at your sides, and relax. Bring all of your awareness to your body. Just think about what you can feel. Feel your feet touching the ground. Feel your bottom sitting in your chair, your head and neck in line with your spine. Now bring your attention to your breath. Notice that you are breathing. Begin to feel your breath moving in and out. Watch your breath, watch it move deeply, slowly, and gently, in and out as your body begins to relax and let go. If your mind wanders off, gently and firmly bring your attention back to your breathing and body awareness practice. Relax and be fully present for fifteen minutes. You will be amazed how this simple practice can make a big difference.

WANT PEACE?
Create it for someone else.

Eknath Easwaren talks about dwelling on oneself as
the root cause of most personal problems. He says, the
more preoccupied we become with our private fears,
resentments, memories and cravings, the more power
they have over our attention. When we sit down to
meditate, we cannot get our mind off of ourselves. With
practice, however, we can learn to pay more and more
attention to the needs of others—and this carries over
directly into meditation. The source is within us. My
judgment or mood is projected onto someone else and
it reflects what I am feeling. It bounces back to me. If I
want to feel peace, joy, and happiness—I need to create
peace, joy, and happiness for someone else.

PAX
ET
BONVM

Closure

....

A LETTER TO THE READER

Resting in my mother's arms

Reverently I walk under a carved stone archway, deep inside secure, walled borders, across an enchanting porch called "the cloistered walk," leading me to my room to settle in for my weekend retreat.

Villa de Matel is a convent founded in 1866, and is beauty defined by peace. Throughout the weekend I begin to soak in its magic. I find a place of no wanting. No longing. Only contentment. Gratitude. Within these walls I find sacred space—and feel the resonance of hours, days, years, a century of prayer. This welcomed refuge provided me a place to heal, to pray, a place to make space in my heart. The silence seemed to support me like the comfort of a good friend. This peaceful oasis made it easier to connect with my divine essence, and rest in a space deep inside myself where I could hear God.

My retreat at Villa de Matel had fairly strict rules: No speaking, using "modest eyes" so as not to catch another's stolen glance, and to keep my intention on creating stillness. And it works. Throughout my silent weekend, a spark is lit. It doesn't light up in a flash, more like a fire begun with well-laid kindling. Just as one would carefully and thoughtfully position paper and twigs to allow enough space for air to get up underneath and support the tender beginnings a flicker of flame needs to ignite.

I have been meditating for about fifteen years, and through my sheer stubborn perseverance of committing to "stay with" my meditation practice, my life is different. I experience life with more respect and gratitude. And occasionally through my meditation practice I get a glimpse of unexpected magic. For me, my weekend in the convent was one of those special moments. Trying to savor it now is so hard to put into words, but the resulting feeling was one I hope you are able to capture as well. My wish in sharing this experience with you is to pique your interest and gently encourage you to make some beginning steps for creating peace in your own life.

During one of the numerous silent meditations over the weekend we came together as a group, sitting and patiently "waiting" for stillness to settle in. We were practicing "centering prayer," the ancient mystical ritual rooted in the earliest Christian monasteries. In this room I was joined with like-minded souls (to whom I would never speak), connected in the pure dedication of showing up. We sat, pooling our collective intention to "prepare our inner room to silence"—to hearing silence and being content with waiting, comfortably faithful of what may or may not appear in this silent space.

Noticing. Noticing a thought, I gently and firmly turn my awareness back and eventually my ordinary mental "static" begins to fade. I am mindful not to resist my thoughts but to expect them, just as waiting for a visitor to turn up at my door. When these "visitors" (my thoughts) turn up, I acknowledge them, and then firmly tell them I am returning my attention to practice. Eventually, the space between my thoughts becomes longer, wider and deeper. And, as I move closer to letting go and surrendering to just "being," I get a glimpse of what feels like bliss to me: *Feeling as if I am a small child—wide-eyed, perhaps five years old, crawling up and into the warm security of my mother's lap. I allow her arms to engulf me, cradle me, and love me. In this place it feels impossible to worry—surrounded by secure freedom, childhood innocence—I am carefree, truly and effortlessly in love with my mother's love for me. I am being held, rocked, and loved from the depths of her heart. A contentment slowly subtly surfaces from a deep, familiar place, a place that appears like a faded memory now recovered. I have no wanting, complete peace and contentment. There is not one thing in the entire world that I long for.*

This experience lasted for about twenty minutes on the clock, but clock time as an illusion. It's difficult to describe my experience as long or short, I only know that when it finished, I missed it. Though I understand the philosophy and guidance of not becoming attached to a blissful meditation experience, I pushed my reasoning aside. I quickly closed my eyes again and tried to get this amazing sensation to come back over me. I could sense everyone else in the room begin to move around and leave. I knew it was time for me to leave, too, but sitting with my eyes closed, I lingered on.

I decided that this is a memory I am choosing to keep. It's one I plan to relish, resting in my mother's secure and loving lap.

You, too, can experience moments of bliss, live a purpose felt life, and respond from a grounded confident place of capacity and generosity. You too, can feel a moment's peace. By now, you have learned to:

- **Use tools of self-awareness,** including body awareness, breathing, and taking the time to relax into a quiet, still space every day.
- **Cultivate the habit** of bringing yourself back into the present moment, a gift that engages you into an immediate experience of gratitude and joy.
- **Dedicate time and attention to self-care,** knowing how essential preventive health care is in creating a place of capacity.
- **Look for good in all things.** Your best treasures are imbedded among your ordinary and mundane daily experiences. These golden threads of priceless experience repeatedly teach you to learn and grow.
- **Recognize serendipitous "signposts"** that always somehow appear and manage to nudge you, reaffirming everything is just as it should be.
- **Teach others best through your own example:** action, thought, deed, and word.

For me, learning how to stay
calm in the midst of chaos,
connecting, returning to that
primordial place anchored deep
within me that the poet T. S. Elliot
called a "still point in a turning
world" has been the key.

And now I pass that key on to you.